hope *love* and me

my journey of choices and second chances

melissa ann

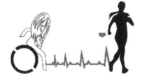

For information about this title or to order other books and/or electronic media, contact the publisher:
Hope, Love, and Me
info@hopeloveandme.org

Library of Congress Control Number: 2018914152

ISBN: 978-1-7329618-1-4

table of contents

To Mom and Dad. I sincerely apologize everything you're about to read is based on actual events. I'm slowly figuring this life out. Thank you for sticking around. I love you guys today and always.

[When it comes to God] We can't run
out of second chances . . . only time.

— ROBIN JONES GUNN

prologue:
the break of dawn

One night changed everything.

I don't remember every teenage thought and emotion I once had. I expected them to diminish with time. But I never expected that one day I would forget what physical touch and independent movement felt like. Yet, this is my now reality. I no longer remember what it feels like to walk, pick something up, or even be able to do the simplest tasks for myself.

My heart was crippled after my first breakup, but that was nothing compared to what I woke up to days later. And to think I thought the previous road was a burden; ten thousand missed signs, and all I needed was a yellow light. I lost hope, I lost love, and I also ended up losing myself.

My physical freedom wasn't supposed to dissolve like this. My body—oh my body. Where do I begin to tell you about everything that is different these days? I've learned acceptance, and I wonder if everybody this many years afterward has. I'm a vibrant 28-year-old, but my age doesn't even begin to count all of the life compressed in my years.

Hope . . . Must we almost lose it to know we are alive? Love . . . Why do we crave it to the point of self destruction? And then there is . . . me. Who am I? Am I the girl that pushed the limits, foresaw no consequences, and took the ordinary for granted? Or am I the woman I am becoming? The one who is learning humility, compassion, and unconditional love? Both. And possibly everything in between.

Don't be mistaken though; I'm no dazzling woman. I've tasted life, I have tasted love, and they have brought me to a remarkable place. My story has been immersed in love, but it has also been touched by tragedy. I wouldn't say my story is either one of those, though.

The morning sun has risen, as it does every morning before a caregiver greets me. The room I call my own circulates with crisp air from the two bedside fans humming. My mind thrives on spontaneity, but most days I rely on routine.

I lie here and try not to think about all the stress that naturally comes when you rely on people for everything. And I'm not just referring to somebody else showing up to a meeting. I'm talking about someone putting his or her own needs aside to show up at your house and pick you up out of bed.

And not even because the world revolves around me, but because I want to be on time to a summer camp I'm scheduled to speak at. I volunteer in the hopes that my story will change other people's lives—so they don't have to go through what I do every day. To live a life that is seen as something "nobody else wants to go through" can damage your mind if you let it. It can, quite honestly, warp your entire existence.

The journey can be burdensome, but I have found peace in its surroundings. I find freedom in nature, and it's tickling my heart at this moment, as I'm anticipating the opportunity to go outside and tell these students all about me. But getting ready is different for me. I need a little help with, well, everything. I'm waiting for a girl who has devoted three years of her life to helping me get out of bed and live life every day.

Out of the corner of my eye, through the window that has the view of the woods surrounding my house, I can see a white Toyota Corolla pulling in. My caregiver has arrived. It's nearing time for me to shower and get some clothes on this body that I'm waiting for God to heal.

The clock hits 7:30; my day has officially started. It's time to find the magic in the mess I wake up to. Join me as I take you through time to experience faith, hope, love, and even different abilities.

1

stuck somewhere between young and adult

It goes like this . . . Mom and Dad are tired of me complaining about my lifelong enrollment in private school. I'm ready to move on to something different and graduate from a bigger school. So finally, halfway through my junior year, I transfer to a public high school. And here's what you don't learn in How to Be a Teenager 101: in actual life, nothing about growing up is easy. More often than not, it's like a continuous loop of someone-please-end-it-now. This manipulating world whispers, "Hey, kid, here are some hormonal private parts that may feel a little good sometimes, but don't screw up!"

I come from a good home. Mom, Dad, and my two brothers keep my reality stable. My mom's love for God is something I've always known. I, too, have always loved God, but it's safe to say I keep Him in the back of my mind. You know, call-out-when-I-need-Him type thing. Although, for as long as I can remember, I've had a strange connection to the light. That connection isn't enough, though. I run to the darkness to stay away from it. I've always found something comforting about the dark, knowing that it can't get any darker. I crave fun, like what I see in the world and entertainment industry.

I'm sixteen, and for my big-girl birthday, my parents bought me a black Toyota Tundra. I'm over the freaking moon about starting a new chapter in life. It's my first day at public high school. I'm wearing a Hollister hoodie, tight sweatpants, hair in a messy bun, and my Walgreens-clearance makeup is on point. I'm feeling all sorts of fresh, pulling into the school parking lot for the first time, driving my truck like it's a Cadillac. There's just one problem . . . I don't know anybody. I'm kind of scared, maybe a little nervous. What about lunch? Who am I going to sit with?

Holler for a dollar, there's a girl here, Brandi, I know from middle school! She was super quiet when we met, but I think I bring out the fire she's got caged up in her petite bones. Back in eighth grade, my version of fun with her was me running up to every house in the neighborhood and pouring Italian dressing on the doorstep while talking Brandi into sprinkling on some shredded cheese midstream. Then we would ring the doorbell and run for our lives. Can I get a "nailed it!" for never getting caught?

A whole month goes by at my new school, and Brandi and I always eat lunch together. It's me, Brandi, her boyfriend, and a few of their mutual friends.

"Who is that really cute guy sitting across from us?" I ask Brandi.

"Um, pretty sure his name is Paul. He always sits there. I think he has a girlfriend."

"Dang, what a bummer. I didn't know I had a 'type' until I saw that."

Brandi laughs, like she always does at what comes out of my mouth. "You're a mess, Melissa."

I've never had a boyfriend. Last year I did have a bad crush on this super-hot guy, but I was too darn nervous to get within girlfriend-striking distance. After my parents gifted me my Toyota Tundra, I spent more time stalking this guy than actually hanging out with him. I let him kiss me a few times, but other than that, I couldn't find the courage to be anything close to what he wanted. Sometimes I am my own worst enemy—but who isn't?

I think this fear of having a boyfriend actually saves me from getting myself into a lot of trouble.

Last year was a year full of sneaking out. My older brother, Chris, has a window close to one of mine. Our house is not ground level, and I somehow always managed to miss the step on to the electrical box and instead would fall from the window and hit the dirt with a *kathud!* Chris would just casually move his blinds and look down at me, shaking his head. He doesn't understand why I never sneak out the front door, which leads directly into his room. Whatever, I crack up and run off. I swear, though, I break my butt every time.

It's not my fault I have this bogus eleven o'clock curfew. Thank God my birthday is coming up in April; that will officially move my curfew to midnight. I literally can't wait. My parents have promised that, every birthday, they'll move my curfew up an hour. This started when I was fifteen, with a ten o'clock curfew. My mom and dad are so annoying. I swear all they want to do is make my life boring. Let's face it, parents can suck.

I stopped sneaking out after getting caught one night with that super-hot crush I mentioned. He and his brother picked me up, and we ended up going to a buddy's house. My heart dropped when I saw my dad's name pop up on my cell phone. THAT was terrifying. Later that night my dad asked me if I'd ever snuck out before this. I instinctively replied, "No, I promise this is my first time."

Little did I know my dad was already on to me. I had left dirty feet marks on the outside of our house below my window—evidence of all the other times I had crawled back up into my room. I had been caught in yet another lie, and I was grounded. I honestly haven't snuck out since.

Thankfully, even with all the trouble I get myself into, I still have two best friends, Kristen and Kaley. I met Kaley through Kristen, and Kristen and I met in middle school. I remember back in those weird years Kristen and I didn't really talk that much. Kristen had a lot of friends, and I never really fit in. My hyperactivity and craze for excitement kept me far too busy to worry about accumulating friends. She would sometimes French braid my hair during lunch break. We didn't dislike each other, but for some reason we never really became friends until the beginning of tenth grade, when I ran into her at the mall. We went to the movies with this boy we mutually knew from school, and after that we have never stopped hanging out.

I don't think Kristen, Kaley, and I have ever even had a fight. On a normal day, we jam out in my truck to a Missy Elliott song or Yung Joc's "Hear Me Coming," moving our bodies to every beat that drops. A few blondes making the best out of the worst. When we have any free time, we basically do everything together. Sometimes we dress up and go on cute date-night dinners. Other times we try and figure out if a party's going on somewhere. Kristen and Kaley go to a different high school than I do, but that doesn't stop us from constantly hanging out. For the most part, they keep me balanced.

hope _love_ and me

I've always been a fearless, living-the-dream type of person— a blonde with a bad-girl personality. I am five feet, five and a half inches tall (every half-inch counts), and I thrive on physical activity. I tend to get a little sassy, and I like to stay on my toes, physically and mentally. Dirt bikes have been a thing in my family for as long as I can remember. With my V-8 Tundra, Yamaha dirt bike, and energetic personality, I like to have fun. So if you spot something with wheels, you just might see me on it.

"No way! You're crazy, Melissa!" my cousin Krista exclaims over the phone.

Krista's dad is my mom's brother, and they live an hour away. I'm desperately trying to get her to come to my side of the world. My brother recently had to replace the hood on his truck, so you know what that means . . . the boys in my family and I are going to rig something up, a stunt we are calling "hood sliding." Basically, we're going to get a long snatch rope, tie it to the back of a dirt bike, and tow each other around while surfing on my brother's old hood.

Krista is a different kind of adventurous than I am. We are both tickled by the outdoors; I just tend to be a bit more careless than she is. I'm always trying to persuade her (only because I choose to ignore all the differences in our interests). I can't grasp why she doesn't enjoy what I do. I know we can't all be the same, but still, we're cousins by blood. The phone call did not end in my favor. She thinks I'm crazy, and sometimes I can't blame her. My dad, two brothers, and I will make this fun nonetheless.

* * *

Life has been treating me pretty fairly. I complain about the normal things: boys, school, parents, and work. I started working as a cashier at a local grocery store when I was fifteen. Between working the register, meeting new people, swinging by the bakery to eat a mouthwatering chocolate-covered strawberry, going outside to get shopping carts, and then maybe hiding in the freezer to cool down, I keep work fun. Do I enjoy it? Most of the time no, but I sure do enjoy picking up my check every Thursday.

One thing my parents have instilled in me and my brothers is that hard work pays off. My parents never come home from work and crash on the couch, needing what some people call "me time." It doesn't matter what stressors work gave them that day, they never bring it home. Instead, they give us as much time as we need. My parents keep most things private between themselves. Heck, I've never even seen them kiss!

I'm at work right now. It's a cold February day, and the clock just hit 12:34. I cannot wait to get off.

Honestly, it would've been a fine shift if my manager hadn't just called me into the office and told me that a customer had complained. They said I was paying more attention to the bagger than I was to them. Really? The only question that should matter is, Paper or plastic? I'm sixteen, and I just want to have fun.

Well, my shift is over. I'm finally off work. Kristen and I are going shopping. Like most high schoolers, we don't have that much extra cash, since the little money we make from our part-time jobs goes to gas and food. Can I be honest? I often steal. Sometimes because I can't afford to pay for it, but most times just because it is a rush. When did I first start stealing? That I'm unsure of, but I do remember stealing the bag that became the carrier for the all other future things I didn't pay for. The bag was on display at Dillard's. And I do apologize for anybody reading this with a sigh. I am an adrenaline junkie, and the rush of getting away with something is exhilarating. What's the worst that could happen anyway?

I'm on my way to Target, and Kristen is driving. I don't even know what I want. I do need a new pair of high heels. Who knows, maybe if I find a cute pair, I will land my first boyfriend.

"What do you need to get, Kristen? Spring break is coming up so quick. Target always has super-cute bathing suits."

"Umm," she says. "I don't really need much, maybe just some makeup. I'll see when we get there."

We're walking around Target, wishing we could buy everything we see, then—oh, my gosh—I see them. A pair of red heels I've seen only in my dreams. One problem, they cost thirty-two dollars. That is ridiculous. That's basically half my paycheck. Why would I spend so much money on a pair of shoes I will probably wear only once? Maybe, just maybe, these could end up in my bag and nobody will notice. I even have with me the infamous bag I stole from Dillard's, and they would fit perfectly in it.

I'm doing it. I need these heels. Kristen has eyeliner and nail polish in her purse.

A man shopping in the lady's department stops us and asks about women's sizing and pants. I'm taken aback. I don't want to chat; I just want to get out of the store.

"We only shop in juniors," I reply quickly. "You might want to ask an employee—they can help you better."

Kristen and I get to the front of the store. We look at each other; something doesn't feel right. But we've gotten this far, and we can't turn back now.

We walk through the first set of automatic doors. Only one more set of doors, and we're home free. Then everything becomes a blur.

Hands grab us and pull us back into the store. Now we're in a bland, white-walled room with store managers and police officers, and we're being searched.

Turns out, the guy who was in the women's section *is* an employee, a loss-prevention one, and he was trying to keep us from walking out of the store with our lifted goods.

So it's actually happened. I can't believe I've finally gotten caught. Ugh, this sucks. Bonus points, though, for getting arrested with one of my best friends. Pretty pumped I have Kristen in handcuffs next to me.

Kristen and I sit in the back of the cop car, side by side. The FM radio must be feeling our situation because we're jamming to Disturbed's "Land of Confusion." We have our "rock out" hands crushing behind our backs and we're belting out the lyrics.

Mom and Dad are in the Cayman Islands at a relative's wedding. I wonder how it's going to play out when they come home and get the shoplifted-and-arrested news. This is going to be, well, interesting.

My criminal record says I've only stolen once, but I've actually done it multiple times. But screw that; jail life is not for me.

Mom and Dad take away my freedom, and my truck. As well as my dirt bike, phone, and EVERYTHING you can think of. I'm allowed to go only to school and work—wouldn't you know it . . . my two least favorite things. Parents are beyond annoying with all their "we were your age once" comments and efforts to be your friend. Yeah, well, friends don't make life suck.

It's hard being a teenager, doing homework and cramming for tests that won't make my day any better, much less my future any better. I'll probably never use the Pythagorean theorem again after high school— what a waste of time. I'm trying to balance doing all this with having friends, having a good time, not getting fired, graduating, and by the way, it'd still be nice to get a first boyfriend.

That last one, the first-boyfriend thing, probably won't actually happen till I'm twenty-nine, if I'm even that lucky. Everybody I know has had at least one boyfriend by now. I'm a junior. Heck, I'm probably the only girl in school who's still a virgin! Maybe I'm exaggerating, but everybody I know has hooked up with a guy at least once. Me? Well, I have kissed a guy or two, but after that, I panic every time. Not exactly while I'm being kissed (come on, I'm not that bad), but afterward I'm gone like a freight train. It freaks me out.

Honestly, the fear of ending up pregnant or left alone with nothing but a broken heart does not sound appealing. So that's how I manage. I run from anything that has potential of leaving me scarred.

It's Friday. School finished at 2:10, and now I'm at work, as usual. It's only a three-hour shift, though. Most of my shifts are short because I'm a minor, and labor laws are strict. Ryan is helping me bag the groceries. He is the same bagger who the customer had complained about me talking to. Right now, I dare someone to complain again. I need to vent.

Ryan's a cool guy. We go to the same school, and we keep each other laughing while on the clock at work. Trust me, it makes the time go by faster. Between customers, I'm venting to him about my grounded life and how relying on Mom or Dad to pick me up from school and work sucks.

Ryan replies, "Why don't you just ask Paul to take you to school?"

"Who's Paul?" I say, carefully handing him eggs to bag.

"Your neighbor. Don't you know Paul? I think we all have the same lunch together. He's going through some stuff with his girlfriend, but you riding to school with him won't be a big deal."

All I can think to myself is, *Oh crap, that's the guy I always see at lunch! Not a big deal? Doesn't Ryan know this guy is gorgeous and that I would get lockjaw just sitting next to him?*

Two years ago, when we moved in to our house, I totally hid in our bushes with binoculars and watched our eye-candy neighbor-boy pressure wash his driveway. My dad had bet me I wouldn't hide in the bushes for a gaze. Pshhh, who wouldn't do it? I sure did, and I liked what I saw. Tall, dark, handsome, he looked like a dream come to life.

Nfsgvnhdcj. Word vomit. I don't know what to say to Ryan.

Somehow I splutter out, "For real. Trust me, I'm not trying to be anything but single. Do you have his digits?"

stuck somewhere between young and adult

"Yep," Ryan replies. "We hang out all the time. Do you want it?"

"What time do you get off? I'm off at seven."

"Yeah, me too," he says.

"No way! Cool, well, my phone is still taken away so I'll call him from yours when we're out of here, if that's cool?"

"Sounds good."

OH, MY GOSH. I think I'm experiencing mild cardiac arrest. What the heck did I just get myself into? What am I going to say? Like, "Hey, neighbor boy, so I screwed up last month and got arrested. By any chance have you got a free passenger seat?"

What a joke!

But I'm at least doing a good job of playing off my nervousness in front of Ryan. Guaranteed if he felt my pulse, he would laugh. But it is what it is. I need this ride. I'm darn sure sick of relying on Mom and Dad.

Ryan and I both clock out and walk out of the store. Not even a second after our feet hit the parking-lot pavement, his phone is up to my ear, RINGING. I look at the screen and, no surprise, it's calling Paul.

Shiiiz . . .

He freaking answers.

"Hello?"

"Hey, Paul. This is Melissa. Not sure if you know we're neighbors? I kind of got into a little trouble and my 'rents took my truck away. I was wondering if I could get a ride to school with you? No worries if not."

He laughs and says that's fine. He tells me to be at his truck at 6:50 Monday morning. I hand Ryan back his phone, trying to look unfazed by what just happened.

Well, the weekend was slower than my great-grandma walking to the bathroom. Finally, the time comes. It's Monday morning. I'm wearing my favorite Alpine Stars red T-shirt and my jeans that grip everything you can imagine.

Technically, there's a house between Paul and me, but that house sits farther back, so really it's just beautifully manicured lawn between us. The clock hits 6:48, leaving me only two minutes to double check my makeup and get to his truck. Rush, rush, rush. Story of my life.

Here goes nothing.

Trust me when I tell you that the walk over would have been uneventful if there hadn't been a hole in the ground that my foot fit into perfectly. Leaves were hiding it, and yeah . . . you get the idea. Down I go, and Paul sees every bit of it.

After wiping off the leaves and dirt, I play off my nervousness with laughter and get in his truck. We don't even make it out of the driveway before he lets me know my zipper is down.

OH, MY GOSH. Can this get any more embarrassing?

Sure can. My zipper isn't down; it's actually broken. What a motherlode of awkwardness; this is going to be my look for the entire day. Ugh, I want to cry. Why must all of this happen the day I get to mingle with my yummy neighbor?

The radio is on, I hear the "Ice Ice Baby" beat, and I can't help but move my body to it.

Paul goes, "Do you know this song?"

"Yeah, of course, I know this song," I say. "It's Vanilla Ice!"

He smiles and says, "I knew you were going to say that. Everybody thinks that when they first hear this song. But this actually came out before 'Ice Ice Baby.' This is Queen—'Under Pressure.'"

"Ohhh, you don't say. I guess one does learn something new every day. Thank you for that information, mister."

He says with a smirk, "No problem."

What I really wanted to say was "Mr. Delicious." Why so cute? Just why?!

I wonder what he thinks of me. I can see myself falling hard for this guy, riding to school with him for the next few weeks and getting to know him. Word has it that his girlfriend actually cheated on him and they are on the verge of breaking up.

Why in tarnation would anybody cheat on him? Granted, yeah, I know only so much about him, but he seems like a really good guy. We actually have a lot in common. We both love all things country, motocross, and playing in the dirt. He too has a Yamaha dirt bike and, keep this between you and me, but I sometimes see him watching me take laps on my two-stroke around our couple of acres. I hope it's not just the bike his eyes are locked on.

A full month goes by. Paul is still taking me to school, but that's coming to an end soon, once my truck keys are back in my hand. When I'm at work, Ryan thinks it's funny to write on little brown paper bags "Melissa loves Paul," or he'll just write Paul's name surrounded by a bunch of hearts.

I play it off. I'd say I'm pretty smooth with comebacks and pretending like I don't crave a chance being with Paul. He and his girlfriend didn't work out. As you can imagine, she doesn't like me for the simple fact that I'm spending time with him. But I'm over here like, Why so bitter? I'm not the one who cheated on him. Seriously though, he's just taking me to school, nothing more than hitching a ride. Would I pass up a chance to go on a date with him? Probably not. Somehow I would have to find the courage to say yes; you can't help who you end up liking. If given the opportunity to date Paul, well, now it's my turn.

The way everything has been playing out has been quite stellar. I guess you could say I got "ungrounded," because I have my truck back. My birthday came and went—April 6. I'm finally seventeen, and things are looking up. I was worried that once Paul stopped taking me to school, our friendship would disappear, too.

Much to my surprise, though, we've started hanging out. Eek.

He texted me and asked if I wanted to go with him to his friend's house. Thank God he asked in a text and not by calling me, because I probably would have been silent for too long. I wouldn't have been able to handle knowing he was on the other end of the line, waiting for my response. But I knew I had to say yes. Why not, right? So I did.

We're driving down a back road I never knew existed. Even though I've lived in this neighborhood for two years now, I haven't done much exploring. I'm hoping Paul can change that for me. We are in his blue lifted Chevy truck, he's driving, and we're making small talk. Mostly he's telling me about his best friend, Brian, who we're going to see, and all of the crazy things they have done together. I've done some pretty crazy things also, mostly involving alcohol, but I don't want to come across as a party girl. I don't think I am one, actually. It's just that if the opportunity presents itself, I tend to get a little wild.

We get to Brian's house. I'm getting out of the passenger side and thinking to myself, *Nailed it!* I actually look pretty cute. I have a little jean skirt on and a tight-fitting Victoria's Secret green long sleeve. As usual, the top is low cut. Meeting new people has never been hard for me, especially when they're random guys I'm not interested in. I have no problem starting up conversations and keeping them going. Brian and

I are talking about the normal things: trucks, dirt bikes, and where the pavement ends.

On the drive home, I'm sitting a little closer to Paul than I was when he first picked me up. I don't want to come off as super interested because, honestly, if the feeling isn't mutual, that would bite. But at the same time, I want him to at least somewhat know I am at risk of falling for him. We pull into my driveway, he gets out of the truck, and before I can even think about how to say goodnight, he gives me a big hug. He's six feet, maybe even an inch or two more than that, and with me at five-five (and don't forget about that half inch), it feels too right.

It's impossible to fall asleep. I can't stop thinking about him. As nervous as guys make me, Paul is different. I feel safe around him.

I've been waiting for love. I want more of him.

2
summer nights and liberties

The transition has been easy. We started off as neighbors; then he took me to school. After he and his girlfriend were officially over, he finally updated my name in his phone. Originally, I was the name of his stepsister, Megan. He said he had to do that because his girlfriend would take his phone and look through it. Now we're full-on friends, and hanging out has become consistent. As the days accumulate, we have gotten closer and closer. I keep anticipating when, or if, he will have the guts to kiss me. Because if you ask me, the flirting hasn't stopped since day one.

I just left a restaurant, picking up wings for him and his friend Mike. I dig Mike. Partly because we have the same last name, but mainly because he's fun to be around. I pull into the driveway, park my truck behind Paul's, and hop out with the wings in hand. As I'm walking to the front door, it opens, and I'm greeted by both Mike and Paul. Paul's parents are on vacation, which explains the open beers on the counter. Free beer, why not. I'm a lightweight anyway, so one is enough for me.

This beer definitely has me feeling some type of way; I'm even more comfortable around Paul. I don't know much about alcohol, but it's making me enjoy every second next to Paul. He grabs my hand and pulls me next to him on the couch. Mike is cracking us up. He's behind the blinds that separate the living room from a little bar behind it. The blinds go from ceiling to floor and are closed, but Mike is on the backside of them jumping in and out. I'm telling you I can't stop laughing; I inherited my loud laugh from my mom. My left shoulder is on Paul's chest. I can feel his heart beating, and I'm imagining for the millionth time what his lips would feel like. I hope he kisses me soon, because I can't take this much longer. My heart just might explode.

It's the next day, and I am in the passenger seat of Paul's truck. He has the sexiest fox-racing sticker on the back window. We are in a parking lot by my job, holding hands. There's a break in the conversation, he pulls me closer, and to my surprise, he puts his lips on mine. This is our first kiss, the one I haven't stopped waiting on. I'm trying to act natural, but all I can think is that I hope I am kissing him right. I am surely not experienced. Even with all my fears, though, nothing has felt better.

Paul is such a different kind of fun.

I'm going to fall asleep tonight feeling over the moon. It's the summer before senior year, and I'm talking to the cutest guy in school. Thankfully, he is not the most popular. To me, though, he is definitely one of the most attractive guys on campus. Trust me, I walk the halls every day, I'm not exaggerating.

It's midnight, and I'm at home in bed. I can barely keep my eyes open. My phone lights up, and the screen says "Paul." The message says, "I don't kiss girls I'm not dating."

Ahhhh! I sit straight up in bed. Does this mean Paul and I are officially dating? Is that what this means? I can't ask him because that's probably a stupid question. He basically just said we are dating, since he just kissed me for the first time! Eeekk. I reply, "Me, neither."

So just like that (at least I'm hoping it's official) I have my first boyfriend. It couldn't be better timing because Kaley has been dating a guy, Kristen is in a new relationship, too, and we are the best of friends. While this year has had its issues because of some of the choices I've made, what a memorable year it has already been. I'm anticipating what else is to come.

I've been over to Paul's house many times, but not once when his parents were there. Tonight, I am almost certain I'm going to meet them for the first time. He told me to head over after work. I make a pit stop at home, ditch the cashier uniform, and put on some normal clothes. I'm just going to drive over because I'm not going to go back home once I leave his house. I pull into his driveway and park my truck right behind his; it feels like a perfect fit every time.

I walk into his house and immediately see his tall, beautiful mom in the kitchen. He must have gotten his height from her. She greets me, and, right off the bat, I can hear her southern accent.

"Hi, sweetheart, nice to meet you. You must be Melissa."

I've never been this nervous meeting someone's parents. But I pull it together quickly and say, "I am. It's so nice to meet you guys. Paul is awesome."

And then his stepdad, Farrell, comes around the corner, and I immediately feel his energetic personality. Thinking the introductions are over, I'm ready to run off to Paul's room, but then Farrell blurts out something he seems to have been waiting to say.

"Bush girl! It's nice to finally put a face to the name!"

Too many shades of red is an understatement. What is he talking about? Bush girl?

I get to Paul's room, and he's dying of laughter. He explains to me that the day I was crawling through the bushes spying on him, I was not as secretive as I thought. Apparently, Farrell and Paul both knew what was going on, and both of them were looking forward to meeting me. I am so embarrassed it's not even funny. I hope at some point they forget about that and call me by my real name.

Time flies with Paul. Every day I can't wait to see which of us is going to kiss the other first. It's everything I have dreamed of, and more. I'm full of a million butterflies, and my heart feels like it's going to burst. My blue eyes have given him permission to run away with my heart; I don't want to live my life with anybody but him, and he knows it.

We've been official for more than a month, and he tells me for the first time that he loves me. I've let go of everything I've ever held on to. I've fallen in love to the point where it feels like there's no return. I've guarded my heart for so long. I've never ever wanted to be "just another girl."

I have completely given my mind, body, and soul to Paul. He has it all. The burning summer nights have seen everything.

He's my tall country boy, and I'm his motocross girl. We're just two kids trying to live out a song. My hands fit so perfectly in his. His are like twice the size of mine, and I love how my hand completely disappears when he is holding it. Every day he wraps his arms around my neck, and I fit my arms around his whole body. There is something about the way he feels, something so comforting about his love for me. I lose my breath when I see that his eyes are all over me. I love living in these moments when our hearts collide.

I doubt I'll ever again be able to say that my neighbor is the love of my life. This feels like a movie. Sometimes we meet at midnight, and sometimes I sneak over to his house after my parents fall asleep. I just want to be everywhere he is. Yes, I started sneaking out again. But this time I can rationalize it. I'm not partying or drinking or putting myself in a dangerous situation. I just want to fall asleep in Paul's bed, next to him. I love sleeping with my favorite person, and his favorite pillow.

I'm in a lusty love . . . wait, did I just say that out loud? I meant to say I'm in love!

My dad wakes up super early for work. I have to set my phone alarm for 4 a.m. so I can leave Paul's house, run down the street, and quickly get up through my window before anyone notices I'm gone. I'll admit, it freaks me out running through the dark by myself. I'll never tell Paul, but I feel better when he walks with me down the road, protected by giant trees. I must be lucky because when I wake up and give him a kiss goodbye, most times he does walk with me, and I feel safe. We've had a couple of close calls, though, hiding behind the big trees, hoping we haven't been caught. But I can't stop until something stops me. I don't want this to ever be over. It's not enough to say, "I need you."

3
where the pavement ends

Senior year starts tomorrow, and I'm still in shock that it's finally come. I can now say I am a senior in high school, with a boyfriend. Somebody pinch me! I can't wait to walk the halls hand in hand with Paul. Things are so good right now. I didn't have many friends when I first transferred junior year, but things are different these days, stepping into senior year.

I took a summer school class this summer to get Economics out of the way, a requirement for seniors. I hated every minute of summer school, except for one part. I met this rad girl named Sammie, and she is freaking hilarious. It took no time for us to become best friends. She's my type of people, no doubt. One day in class she whispered under her breath that she had the answers to the test, and after that, we started hanging out, and we haven't stopped. I kid you not, the first day we hung out, we were actually skipping out of summer school, exploring some random back road that ended up being a private driveway. She started reversing top speed and got her Hyundai Tiburon stuck in a ditch. I had to phone Paul and ask him to pull us out with his truck. It was worth the big hug I got from him afterward.

Did I mention I like to put the *good* in good times? Senior year is going to be epic.

I'm digging my schedule this year. The only required class I have is English. The rest are electives. My favorite class is Wood Shop. I'm the only girl in it, and, boy, do I love that. I get to build stuff all year, and the best part is that it's sixth period, the last class of the day.

The first day of senior year came and went. It stinks because Paul and I don't have lunch together. So instead, we're going to meet randomly between classes. I guess a quick kiss is better than nothing.

Now it's the morning of the third day of senior year. Last night Sammie and I hung out with one of our mutual friends, Taylor. The three of us decided we were going to take school to the next level today. As usual, I am the driver, so first I pick up Sammie, then Taylor. When Taylor comes out of her house, she grabs something out of the bushes and hops into my truck. That something is a bottle of vodka. Not going to lie, I prefer beer over liquor. I know that technically I'm underage, but seriously, everybody in high school drinks. We're skipping first period, and I'm driving around while Sammie and Taylor drink. I try the tiniest sip, but, ew! No chaser, I can't do it. Liquor really is not my thing.

We pull into a Chick-fil-A parking lot because no doubt Sammie and Taylor need to eat something after drinking almost the whole bottle. Not to mention, I practically live at Chick-fil-A, and I'm starving. Taylor is sitting in the passenger seat, and Sammie is sitting between us, the center console flipped up.

"Ready to chow down, ladies?" I say, with nothing but good food on my mind.

Taylor slurs, "Yeahhhhhhh, let's do this."

Then it happens so fast. Taylor opens her door to get out, but within half a second, she's on the pavement screaming that she's dislocated her shoulder. Oh, my gosh, seriously? I love these girls, but this isn't exactly fun when you are the only sober one. Totally wish Taylor had grabbed beer instead.

We get inside the restaurant, eat, and then drive to the student parking lot. Second period is about to start, and we only have a few minutes to get to our separate classes. Sammie and I both have Environmental Science. Taylor is one year younger, still a junior, and has Algebra.

"What do I do with this little bit of vodka left?" I ask them.

"Uhhhh . . ." Sammie slowly gets out of the truck and starts cracking up. "Just throw it away. Or if you want, you can have it. I'm so drunk right now."

Oh, boy. I don't want to waste this vodka. Maybe Sammie will drink the rest of it after class? Or maybe I can give it to someone else? Whatever, I grab an almost-empty bottle of vitamin water in my truck, chug the last of the water, then dump the rest of the vodka in it. It's maybe only a shot or two, but it's not easy getting alcohol at our age. I don't want to waste it.

Sammie and I get to second period, and we're chilling for about ten minutes when the school administrator pulls us out of class. All I can think is, CRAP. I have the freaking vodka in my backpack! Oh my gosh, what do I do? Should I run for it?

As we're being escorted down the hall, I blurt out, "I really have to use the bathroom. Can I please pee really quick?"

This lady must know what's up because she says "No."

We get to the front office and, no surprise, they search my backpack. They immediately find my vitamin water bottle. They open it up and smell it, and then they look at me. "What is this?" they say. All I can think is, *Really? Should I answer that sarcastically? What the eff.*

They call my parents, and my mom meets me at school. She is absolutely livid.

Because I had alcohol in my backpack, the administrator and security guards are now searching my truck. I had completely forgotten until now that I have a couple cans of beer from a while back under the back bench of my truck. Funny how you remember stuff like this at all the wrong freaking times. They're trying to lift up the back seat, where the cans are hidden, but thankfully I guess my Tundra is a little different than most vehicles. My back bench opens from where the backrest is and then you pull up. They keep trying to pull it from the bottom of the front bench, and nothing is budging. So I tell them I've never lifted it up—I'm not sure how to do it. They find nothing in my truck, thank God, and I'm sent home from school.

All three of us—me, Sammie, and Taylor—get a ten-day suspension with possible expulsion.

This sucks because the three of us—what we like to call the tripod—just started hanging out a lot. Between getting in trouble with alcohol at school and totaling Sammie's Tiburon this past summer (which, by the way, I call Turbino—long story) her parents have banned us from hanging out. To be honest, I highly doubt that's going to stop us.

Paul is a little aggravated, too. He thinks Sammie and I make stupid choices when we're together, and he doesn't like us hanging out, either. Let me give you some background info. My interest in motocross has always helped me find guy friends. Well, now that Paul is my boyfriend, he doesn't feel comfortable with me hanging out with guys he isn't friends with, which is normal. I mean, I guess I understand because if it was the other way around, I would be uncomfortable with him hanging out with other girls. But other than Kristen and Kaley, I don't really have many female friends.

Sammie, on the other hand, has been a cool change of pace and so much fun to hang out with. While, yes, she is a girl, she also admitted to me one night in my room after summer school that she has tried to like guys, even date one, but she thinks she is more interested in females. Some people might be turned off by that confession, but I couldn't care less. I see her heart instead of her orientation. I have fun with her in such a different way. It's funny because when she told me her dad was a local pastor, all I could think was, *Wow, sounds like a movie script where the daughter goes against her family's religious beliefs.*

But all I know is, they support and love her no matter what. At the end of the day, that's all we can do.

4
one more chance

"I promise, Mom. I'm not a bad kid," I say. I'm trying to persuade her that this vodka incident was a first, and last, mistake.

"Well, Mel, you're not giving us any positive reinforcement. All we ask is that you go to your classes, do well, and tell us the truth." My mom pushes her hair out of her face.

In my head I'm thinking, *That's not entirely true! That's not all they want.*

My parents never leave me alone, all day, every day. There's always something I'm not doing right. Don't get me wrong: they have given my brothers and me more in life than we could ever imagine. It's just so tedious being a teenager.

Sammie, Taylor, I, and our parents had to meet with the school board to discuss any further punishment. They actually asked us why we did what we did. What a ridiculous question. Obviously, we are trying to live out senior year.

It went well. I guess they saw a little bit of light in our eyes and granted us another chance. All of us will graduate as planned. The only consequence is that we have to check in with a drug and rehab counselor. It's required only periodically throughout the school year, just to make sure we stay on the straight and narrow.

Glad that's over. My parents for the most part believe that I honestly wasn't drinking that morning; they just told me I need to make better choices about the people I hang out with. I may lie often to get away with little things, but I really was sober that morning. After leaving school the day we were caught, I drove down some back road in the woods. I grabbed those few beers I had forgotten were under my seat and threw them as far as I could. I was so mad at myself. My heart knows some of the choices I make are wrong, but I think I get too easily caught up in the destructiveness of trying to have fun.

I don't care, though. Never once have I been a bad person.

August is not my month this year. I have excruciating pain in my lower stomach. My mom and I go to the pediatrician, and he sends us to the hospital for possible appendicitis. I don't even know what the heck that is. The doctor did tell me, though, that the appendix is something I can live without. How strange is that? To have body parts we can live without? I'm really hoping this stomach pain isn't anything more alarming.

I'm at the hospital getting observed, and this guy literally just asked (with my mom right next to me!) if I am sexually active. I just lost my virginity this month, but there's no way I'm going to say that in front of her! Plus, it's not like I can say, "Hey there, guy, can I just speak with you outside of the room?" So instead I say, "I mean, I've tried?"

As expected, Mom's eyes get huge. I guess that was enough of a yes because I'm escorted to the back of the hospital for a pregnancy test. My heart is in my stomach. There's no way I'm pregnant, I JUST lost my virginity. This can't be real . . .

An angel must be on my side because the test is negative. A scan shows I have full-blown appendicitis with possible rupture. Surgeons take me to an OR, they inject me with anesthesia, and one of them tells me to count to ten. My memory after saying three is completely gone.

Everything went as well as it could. My appendix did not rupture, but they said any longer and it would have been worse. I'm in the hospital for a couple days for monitoring. There's no way Paul can see me like this, no makeup on. Our relationship is still too new for that, I would say. I feel more confident when I have fresh powder on and eyelashes that almost touch my eyebrows.

After fully healing and getting released from the hospital with nothing but a scar by my left hip, I'm back in action.

I've toyed with the idea that maybe this appendicitis was a wakeup call. Maybe God doesn't want me on the route I am on. Earlier this summer, my doctor put me on birth control for menstrual-cycle regulation. This almost-pregnancy scare has faded, and I figure at this point what's lost is lost. It's not that I don't care about my body or that I plan on doing what the world calls "sleeping around." I'm just so in love with Paul that being with him feels like a normal part of our committed relationship, right?

It's kind of funny because when Paul first met my mom at the beginning of the summer, he was sitting on the end of my bed in my room. She walked in quite quickly, introduced herself, and then made it very clear that her daughter is a virgin. She said that it better not be his intention to change any bit of that. I was so embarrassed! All I could think was, *Really, Mom?!*

I hadn't even told Paul yet that I'd never been sexually active, but he sure found out that day. My mom has always taught me to respect myself, which I do, but nothing about what I do with Paul feels wrong. I've never felt like this before.

✳ ✳ ✳

A few months slip by, and it's a Monday morning. I'm skipping first period, again. It's not that I don't like my interior-design class, it's just that sometimes breakfast with friends takes priority. I'm at Chick-fil-A hanging with Sammie, Taylor, and her friend Ashley. It's a little bit of a weird morning because everybody knows something I don't. I'm over here like, "Well, what is it?" Nobody wants to say anything because I guess everybody knows it's going to end up changing everything.

Ashley takes a break from chewing and clears her throat. She says, "Melissa, there is something I need to tell you."

I'm all ears.

She tells me it's about Paul.

"Wait, what?" I say. I can hear my voice shaking. "Please don't tell me something bad." But nothing about her face tells me it's going to be good news.

"Please don't get mad at me, Melissa, but I need to let you know that he cheated on you. My friend Sarah told me she hooked up with him this weekend at Brian's house."

I can't breathe. She's got to be lying. There's no way Paul would ever do something like this to me. We've only been dating a few months. He always says he loves me. Why would he do that? Why would he do this to me?

Nothing comes out of my mouth, just tears flooding my face.

All I can get out is, "Are you sure?"

She's sure. She is absolutely sure.

I get in my truck; I want to go home. I can't go to school. I have to tell my mom what happened so she'll let me stay home. This is the stupid gossip you hear about in the school hallways. This isn't supposed to happen, not to me. I do everything for Paul. I've given him everything. Why would he lie to me? Why would he touch somebody else? I am so angry.

My mom's dark-gray Nissan Armada is in the driveway. She's in the kitchen, and I walk in bawling. All she wants to know is what is wrong, and why am I not in school. I tell her the whole story. I ask her to please not make me go to school. Please don't make me see him. She keeps saying I have to go to school. I'm on the home stretch. High school is almost over. She comforts me and tells me to call her if it gets worse, but to please make it to school.

I confront Paul through text messages before I have to see his face. I ask him why he would do this to me. It's hard to even wrap my head around it. He basically turns it around and makes me look like the stupid one. He calls me a couple of words I'll never forget and tries to make me feel like I was in the wrong for even asking. Of all people, he should know what it feels like to be cheated on. Of all people, he should never be the one to make that mistake. I have done nothing wrong.

Paul and I break up . . . but not for long. To be honest, it has only been two or three days. I never would have guessed dating a neighbor would be this difficult. It's nothing less than love-hate. When things are good, it's got to be better than any other kind of relationship, but, oh, when things are bad, it is miserable.

As soon as I walk into Paul's room, he picks me up and kisses me more times than I can count. In my heart I know he couldn't have cheated on me. He says she made it up; she's been wanting to hook up with him for the longest time. It sucks when your heart is in so deep, vulnerable to every kind of pain, yet unable to fully escape the rush that comes with it. Paul burns through the midnight hours in a way I didn't know was possible. I'm not giving up on him, us, or how far we've come. The more I try to find out the truth, the more I end up losing. So I guess I'm in it for the long haul. I hope he is, too.

He stole my heart. There's a fire in his touch, and that's what keeps me hanging on.

His dark eyes dare me to toy with danger. We have this heat between us; I can't find the will to break away from it. Usually I would run from something that has the risk of burning me, but this relationship has brought me to a place I don't want to leave. Maybe it's because I've waited for him. Maybe it's simply because we are young. But neither one of us can be so easily defined. So maybe it's because we are so passionate about each other at this moment in time. Actually, I don't care what it is. I've tried so hard to take things slowly with him; I have, but I've lost the desire to be anything other than changed.

We have too much tension between us. He tells me how badly he wants me, and I would be okay if I never heard anything else. The text messages and unfinished conversations between us keep me on edge, anticipating the next time he grabs me. I run to his house most nights with this tight feeling in my chest, and I wonder what's going to happen after he pulls me through his window.

Most of the time I can't tell you whose clothes come off quicker. Other times he has this pause about him that makes my mind run faster than a bullet train. I try to read him and figure out what he's going to do. Somehow, he makes me love him more every single time his chest leaves mine and we separate.

Not much in this town rocks me the way that he does. I would say we have the average high school relationship. We bicker and fight about the small things, and even break up frequently. But the away time from each other is minimal. Even when we fight and have a fallout at night, the next day on campus we come back together.

He picks me up, all good-looking in his truck, and somehow I never stay in the passenger seat. I always end up sitting right beside him. I slide on over, and he makes sure there isn't any room to get closer. He feels like a giant when I'm next to him, but such a gentle one. Something about the heat of his body next to mine feels so normal and makes me glad he's the only guy I've given in to. I tell him time and time again that I just want him. I want him to be the only one.

I know I could be a better girlfriend to him though. I enjoy going out without him. I'm not unfaithful, but I like to stray. I like to do things on my own terms. I will admit I have a problem with not including him a lot of the time. It's hard because the fact of the matter is, my best friends are at a different public high school. I tend to get distracted by them and their friends, and many times I leave Paul out of the picture. I'm not doing it intentionally, I honestly just get distracted. He takes it really hard, though. A couple of times he has called me crying because I went off to a party or am hanging out and I didn't include him.

He hates it when I go out and the only way for me to get back home is to drive drunk. Actually, he hates when I drive, period. He says I'm too careless and that it's stupid how I drive. So how do I drive? Well, I like speed. I love my truck's V-8 engine, I love getting places fast, I love feeling like I own the road and that nothing can stop me.

To be clear, I don't drink and drive that often. All I'm saying is, sometimes I have no other way of getting home. And no way would I call my parents for a ride. Then I'd have to tell them that I went somewhere different than where I told them, or even that I went where they thought but I ended up drinking. They would absolutely ground me, take away my dirt bike, and take my truck keys out of my hand. My world would shatter.

Who the heck wants to be grounded? I've had enough of that. I like to go out. I like to mingle with people my age. Sometimes I like to drink, and truth be told, I probably drive more cautiously after a few cold ones.

5
barely legal

Senior year couldn't have gone by faster. It's on the verge of coming to an end—it's already another April 6. Today I turn eighteen. EIGHTEEN! Legally an adult! Wow, I can't believe it. This means the next big thing is graduation, and then hopefully moving out. Paul and I are in the middle of a fight right now. I'm almost thinking he planned this one. It's funny because we weren't fighting around his birthday, but by my birthday, a fight breaks out. Maybe he doesn't want to celebrate with me, or maybe something is bothering him. Either way, tonight I'm single. I'm not saying that in a way like I want to be promiscuous or anything, but regardless, I've got no one to check in with. My parents are out of town for the weekend, and I didn't want to go with them since it's my eighteenth birthday and a Friday night. Hello, don't they know I want to party?

School is over for the day, and Kristen is at my house. We're in my room getting ready for our big night. I got my hair highlighted earlier today, and last week I picked up the cutest, tight-fitting, short pink dress to wear. Do we have plans? Not really. We're going to have a couple of guy friends over tonight and see what else is going on later. We slide a delicious frozen pizza into the oven, and once we're done eating it, we will see what the night holds. I still can't believe I'm finally eighteen.

I'm straightening Kristen's hair when she jumps up, scaring the bejeezus out of me, and says, "Oh, my gosh, Jon just texted me. Do you want to head to his house?"

"Geez, dude, you're lucky I didn't just burn you." I'm laughing. "Freaked me out! Yeah, let's head over."

We get into her Toyota Celica and head over. Jon's fifteen minutes from my house, so it's not a bad drive. As soon as I get out of Kristen's car, Jon says "Happy Birthday!" and gives me the biggest hug.

"What's shaking, Jon, other than my butt later!" I crack up and wrap my arms around him.

"What are you guys doing for the big eighteen?" He smiles. God, he has the whitest teeth.

I tell him we've got some buddies heading over in a little bit. They will bring the beer, and we've got the pizza covered. OH, MY GOSH! The pizza!

"Kristen! We freaking left the pizza in the oven! We have to go!" I'm screaming and busting up at the same time. We are so forgetful.

We jump back into her car, and the whole way home we can't stop laughing. Of course we have to pass Paul's house to get to my driveway, and I notice that he's not home. He should be with me tonight. I'm a little aggravated. Kristen tells me to brush it off—he's the one missing out, not me.

We walk into my house, and it smells like the place is on fire. We open the oven, and what was a frozen pizza is now literally the size of my hand and blacker than the oven it is sitting in. Haha! It wouldn't be a fun birthday without our usual nonsense.

The guys come over. We're all drinking beer and playing games. I get the music going with surround sound, and the beats are bumping like they should be. A few fun hours go by, but I seem to be getting more and more emotional. Unfortunately, since I'm closest to Kristen, my emotions get shoved at her. It's not that I'm upset with her. I just feel broken that Paul isn't around for my big birthday. I didn't even get a "Happy Birthday!" from him at all today. I was there for his, and it just doesn't seem fair. The night ends with tears, but thankfully like after most nights I cry, I wake up the next morning feeling refreshed. I hope I can start eighteen off that exact way—refreshed.

Being a teenager is kind of like, well, not necessarily having nothing to do, just not sure what to do.

My friends and I drive around 24/7, texting people, waiting on replies, and trying to figure out the next adventure. Plenty of times when we're driving through the streets, we make it to a stop sign, then just turn around and start driving the other way. Driving and listening to music, looking for the next freedom.

I go to parties every once in a while. If I'm invited, I usually tag along with Kristen, Kaley, or Sammie. We usually have a beer or two, mostly because it's just something to do. Out of my variety of friends, I'm definitely the most fearless and wildest. I'll be the first one to try something new, or the first one to bust out a dance move. Other than the normal female insecurities, not much freaks me out. I talk like a sailor and, to be honest, I really just do whatever I want. People have always told me I'm manipulative. I don't even realize that I am sometimes, but when people continuously tell me that I am, it must be true. I'm not even going to lie, though: I do end up getting my way a lot.

People don't call me to go to the movies or just to hang out and chat. If my phone rings, it's because they want to get crazy. I love adrenaline. I love playing in the dirt. And I love making other people laugh. If I have to break my arm to get somebody to giggle, well, then you just might see me wearing a cast the next day. Fun is in my blood. It's who I am.

Personally, when I'm alone and have nothing to do, I love to just cruise in my truck. High school gets old. It's all about who is cool, who's not, what's in, what's not. I guess that's life in general, but the pressure of it all is not my jam. I'm a pretty simple person. I like to wear my fishing shoes. I like to wear holey jeans or short cut-off jeans and tank tops. I do doll up and get girlie plenty, but I just don't focus on constantly trying to fix and better the way I look. Don't get me wrong: I'm still a self-conscious teenager. Living in today's world, it is extremely difficult to not be self-conscious when you're constantly surrounded by comparison. I'm anticipating, though, that once I grow up a little bit and grow into who I am, the self-consciousness will disappear. That's the plan, anyway.

As for now, life is all about getting high school over with and trying to make things last with Paul. Not to mention the other things that are still important, like balancing work and friends.

Paul and I are consistently back and forth; I think lately I start most of the fights. I don't even really know why. In a weird way, it's kind of an adrenaline rush trying to stay together. We have such a good time when things are going well. But I hate seeing his truck next door when my mind wants nothing to do with him. There's no way of escaping the fact that he is literally right there.

Overall, it's been a great year with him.

Senior year couldn't have been more fulfilling. I went to so many parties, tried so many new foods, and I can't even begin to count all the dates Paul and I went on. Not to mention all of the times I got him so mad at me, resulting in short breakups and somehow ending up back in his bed. Life would have been peachy if I had stopped back-talking to my parents, getting myself into lots of trouble. Other fond memories of senior year include all the days of school I skipped, every new adventure Sammie and I went on, all of her lesbian friends I became really good friends with, the clubs our fake IDs got us into, spring break with Kristen, my first trip to Ireland, prom, and the trip to the cheap hair salon that ended up frying my hair. That same night I met a lifelong friend, Will. He has a passionate love for motocross and God.

What's next? Well, it includes a cap and gown.

I park at the arena for graduation, then I get out the duct tape and pack of beach balls I purchased on the way. I know they'll search me before I go in, so that's why I'm keeping the beach balls deflated and duct taping them to the inside of my upper thigh. I want today to be memorable for everybody.

So far my plan is working out perfectly. I am sitting in one of the last rows in the back, so nobody but the audience can see what I am doing.

My nana and her sister, Aunt Maura, flew down from New York to watch me glide across the stage and grab my diploma. I actually have quite a few family members who live in New York. I was born there, but my mom and my biological dad split up when I was a baby. We left when I was six months old, but I do fly back and visit everyone at least once a year. I love that side of the family. I always tell them that the lucky side of me is Irish!

Paul and I have been fighting on and off since we got back together after the last day of high school. At graduation while we're waiting in line to walk, I hug him and tell him that I love him. He holds on to me tight and kisses my forehead so many times I almost forget to get back in line. I didn't want to let go because something inside of me keeps burning, like we both know this isn't going to work. I know he loves me. We just can't figure out how to get along.

It has been a rocky summer with him. A rocky year in general. We've met more times than I can count at the 7-Eleven right around the corner from our houses to fight so our nosey parents can't eavesdrop. Even those parking spots are worn out. I'm so glad high school is over, but the one thing I do miss about my senior-year days is that they brought Paul and I back together. Even though we live next door to each other, it's still hard to make us work.

I decide to take a trip to New York, not only to visit family but also to get my mind right. High school is over, college is starting in two months, I'm eighteen and barely legal. This is my life, this is my coming-of-age, but I don't even know who I want to be.

The trip to New York was good. I love seeing my nana. She is sunshine in my life. Plus, seeing all my Irish aunts, uncles, and cousins is always nice. It's cool to have family all over the place. When it was time to fly back home, Paul wanted to pick me up from the airport. As I was leaving the terminal, I saw him smiling like the first time he told me his name. As soon as I got close enough, I jumped into his arms and held on tighter than ever.

Even though Paul and I have been together for a year, my heart still drops when I'm with him. His truck used to be filled with my laughter. Now it's silent and feels empty. This car ride home is nothing but sorries. I don't know exactly where I went wrong, but I want Paul to know I am sorry even for the things I'm not aware of. It's a hard pill to swallow, but I think we are both sick of trying. You can only try something so many times before you have to face that it's just not working. I don't want things to be over, but at the same time, I know Paul is burned out. Neither one of us knows what we're going to do with our future, but a future together does not look promising. This whole summer was spent together and apart. We fight. We make up. We keep craving each other, but never at the same time. All that has filled me with a lot of doubt. I wonder how Paul can love me so much, only to turn around and act like he doesn't care at all. I wonder if I'm just not enough. He no longer gets emotional; I've gone the other way and am getting more emotional every day.

6
a path to nowhere

Fearless is still my middle name, but now I'm leaning a little bit more toward careless. Paul and I put an end to the chaos. We ran out of options to make us work. I can only climb into his bed so many times. I've gotten too cocky for him, and he's too angry with me. But our relationship was mind-blowing, and something I would never change. I'll never forget his intensity and the rush of emotions he gave me when his skin touched mine. I have yet to get drunk enough to get him off my mind.

I put all my memories of Paul's and my past year in a box and placed it in the back of his truck. I hope he never throws it away. I had to get rid of all the things that reminded me of him, so I tell myself not to fall apart if he has to do the same.

I'm still working at the grocery store half a mile from my house, and I'm all registered for classes at the local community college. Kristen is going to a university three hours south, and Kaley is going to one two hours north. I don't know what I'm going to do without them. The only good news is that Kristen recently introduced me to Lee-Anne. Oddly enough, I actually was on a rowing team with Lee-Anne back in freshman year. We lost contact after my parents pulled me off the team because my grades weren't good enough. Lee-Anne and I were both coxswains due to our petite bodies, and I would say we had one heck of an experience. I'm thinking now it's time for a different kind of fun.

She and her boyfriend just broke up, too. What a small world. Just like Paul and me, they couldn't make things work with high school over. And even worse, he left her for another girl. I don't know if Paul left me for another girl, but I did hear he has been hanging out with this other blonde chick. That only fuels so much of the anger I have been holding on to. We literally just broke up, and he's already with another girl? I swear I will break through his window I've been sneaking into for the last year and give him a few words dipped in fists if I find out anything else. Lee-Anne and I both gave everything to these boys, and they just changed their minds.

It's another hot day. I had to work for six hours, but now I'm off and lying in my bed, staring at my phone, hoping for a message from Paul. I really want to hear from him, but I know it's not going to happen. I've had such bad dreams lately. Every dream ends with me being stuck somewhere. Whether that's under something collapsing, near an object burning, or my heart sinking. I just want a peaceful night's rest. I really want to sneak into Paul's window like I used to and just crawl into bed with him and pass out. I want to wake up again with butterflies in my stomach. I stopped by the store after work to buy chocolate Häagen-Dazs ice cream and a couple of DVDs that were on sale. Looks like it's just me and my TV tonight.

A couple of love movies later and I'm wondering whether it's the ice cream or my heart that feels colder.

What I was hoping would be a full night's sleep was only a few hours because I was woken up by a dream that was more real than anything I've ever dreamed before. It's one in the morning, but I have to call Kristen.

"Hello?" Kristen answers groggily.

"Kristen!" I'm ready to spit it all out. "I just had the craziest dream I think I've ever had, and I think I know what I want to do when I grow up!"

"Melissa . . . you just woke me up. Can you please tell me in the morning? I'm exhausted."

"I have to tell you now. I've never had a dream this real in my life." I'm practically begging her to listen.

"Okayyyy, fine."

"I was at this high school. I was speaking to the students. There were thousands of them listening to me. I was talking about drinking and driving and doing drugs—"

"But you don't do drugs, Melissa."

"Yeah, I know, but the students were getting it. They were actually listening to me. I think I really want to do something like that when I grow up."

She chuckles. We both do. I hang up the phone and go back to sleep. When I wake up the next day, I don't give the dream a second thought.

You could say my mind is still a bit scattered. Every morning I can't help but play songs Paul loves. I go to work and come home every day with tears streaming down my face. Not a day goes by when I don't see Paul's house or truck and wonder if he misses me. I argue with myself that he doesn't miss me because he never responds to my texts. Well, sometimes he replies, but our conversations never go anywhere positive. He ends it by telling me that I'm disgusting and a few other words I'm trying to forget. I don't know why he won't just let us be together and work things out.

Apparently, I've made him hate me. Or it's just his way of moving on. I'll never know. But what he's failing to understand is, I would do anything to have him back in my life. I miss him. I know that most high school relationships don't work out, but I thought we would be different. Isn't it normal to think that you're going to be the exception?

I'm trying my best to cover up the fact that I miss him by going out as much as possible. From observing other singles, it seems that going out and staying busy helps you forget the person who burned you. So that's what I'm doing. I'm spending as much time as possible with Kristen, but sometimes she has boyfriend obligations, so I make other plans. I have been hanging out with Lee-Anne a lot, and some random people from high school.

Although Kristen and her boyfriend are still doing well, tonight is a girls' night. Both she and Lee-Anne are sleeping over at my house, and, of course, I spend part of the time arguing with Paul through text messages. He tells me that everything I ever gave him—all the notes I wrote him and all the things I drew for him—are in his garbage by the street. I look at Lee-Anne and Kristen and say, "Are you kidding me?" So the three of us walk out my front door and go to his trashcan and, yes, we dig through it. He lied. Nothing is in there. Nothing from me anyway. I can't stand the stupid games he plays.

The next night Kristen, Lee-Anne, and I are getting together at Lee-Anne's house because her parents are out of town. That last little detail gives us the opportunity for an open house. No precise plans, but the three of us are pretty excited to see where the night takes us. We are thinking we're going to head about thirty minutes east, near a university where there are lots of bars and clubs that are known for letting underage kids in. Exactly what I need to keep my mind busy. Lee-Anne completely agrees.

At Lee-Anne's house, we're getting ready to put our plan into action. Lee-Anne just found a bottle of vodka in her cabinet, and I am on social media updating some stuff. I'm changing my relationship status to single, rearranging some pictures, and dancing to T.I.'s song "Whatever You Like," because that's my jam. All three of us take a couple of shots and start dancing on each other. The clock hits eleven; it's time to get in my truck and head out for a night of adventure.

We get to this club and immediately make friends with the bouncers. I'm goofing off, helping one of them check IDs. I'm having the time of my life; I show the bouncer my ID, laugh, and say, "This is definitely a fake."

He doesn't care. Tonight, my name is Samantha Forbes, and I'm 22. As long as we have an ID, that's all they care about. Lee-Anne looks like she is getting suffocated dancing with one of the other bouncers, so Kristen and I pull her away, and we all head to the dance floor. What a night. There is something thrilling about feeling free. There's something so peaceful about pain dissipating, or at least being numbed.

At this point, though, we have surpassed tipsy and are all leaning more toward drunk. It's time to head out.

We get in my truck. I've always been a pretty fearless driver, but once I have alcohol in my system, I think I own the road. I'm only going a few miles over the speed limit, but I'm being a little reckless. I don't even realize I'm over the curb, off the road, and literally in between the trees. Somehow I don't hit anything. Kristen is hanging her head out the passenger window, throwing up and screaming for me to slow down. The alcohol has really messed her up. Lee-Anne and I are laughing as I pull into her neighborhood. We make it back safely, like we always do.

As soon as we get in the driveway, Kristen runs right to the bathroom and keeps on vomiting. We're in the bathroom with her, trying to persuade her that the bed will be a much more comfortable place to sleep. I keep trying to tell her she will feel better. She keeps saying no, she doesn't want to leave the toilet, so Lee-Anne and I just head to her bed and crash.

When we wake up the next morning, the first thing we do is check on Kristen.

"Oh, my gosh," she says. "I feel like absolute crap."

"Dude, Kristen, you were throwing up like crazy last night. What the heck happened?"

"Am I alive?" she says with her lips looking drier than a raisin.

"I sure hope," I say. "I'm not quite sure how we made it home. I was all over the road. Kristen, you were sick to your stomach in my truck. I still can't believe we didn't crash."

Kristen says that last night she drank whatever people bought her, and she thinks she mixed too many different kinds of alcohol. I don't know much about that, but it sounds right. We all need food so badly, so we head to a café to find something to cure our hangovers.

I order a tomato mozzarella salad, but somehow they forget the mozzarella. How can they forget one of the only two ingredients on the salad? I have no idea, but I don't even realize the mistake until we get back to Lee-Anne's house. I don't have time to run back, get it fixed, and eat with them. I have to be at work soon, and I need to get home and get my uniform on. Thankfully, it's only another six-hour shift today. I already can't wait to get off. Death probably feels better than I do right now. The aftermath of alcohol is not my friend.

The time here at work is going by so slowly, as it does every time I want it to go by fast. It's crazy how that works. When you want time to slow down and go at a steady pace so you can take every bit of a moment in, it flies by. But when you want to rush time, oh, how it seems to go even slower.

Well, I'm trying to hide my phone in the drawer below the register so I can text Lee-Anne and Kristen; maybe they'll want to get together again tonight. Kristen says she and her boyfriend are going out to dinner. So that's a no-go for her. Lee-Anne, on the other hand, said she's free and would love to grab food. I'm trying to low-key laugh as I text her, "I hope wherever we go eat tonight doesn't mess up my order like our lunch excursion did."

I'm clocking out now and getting ready to head home. Not long after I pull into my driveway, so does Lee-Anne.

We're getting ready in my room. We went shopping the other day, and I bought two black tank tops with white writing on them. One of them says "Good Girls Gone Bad" with a bunch of motocross stuff around it. The other one says "F*** Love" with guns, knives, and grenades spelling out the letters of that F word I so love to use. I think I'm going to wear that one. It says exactly how I'm feeling right now.

I'm putting one of my zip-up hoodies over it so my mom doesn't say anything about my top being too low cut. What can I say? If you got it, you got it.

My mom and Aunt Debbie are sitting at the dining room table talking, and I have to walk by them to get out of the house.

"Lee-Anne and I are going to head out to dinner," I say. "At the moment, we are not sure if we're going to do anything else afterward, but I will definitely let you know if we do. Is that okay?"

Aunt Debbie says, "Melissa, how come we never see you anymore?"

I giggle. "Aunt Debbie, come on. I'm eighteen. High school is finally over, and I'm just trying to go out and have fun."

"Okay," she says. "Please make more time for us. You know we love you."

I tell her I will, and my mom tells me to be safe tonight.

Lee-Anne and I get in my truck and decide to head to Taco Bell. I can count on one hand how many times I've eaten here, so I figure why not switch it up. I order three tacos and a side of rice. I haven't eaten since that café confused my lunch order, so I'm pretty hungry. Food and I get along way too well.

Lee-Anne and I are sitting at a little booth right next to the front entrance. Both booths on either side of the table are only long enough to fit one person. As we're eating, practically inhaling our food, we are both texting people, trying to figure out if anything is going on tonight. We have a couple of options.

One of my buddies from high school, Hawthorne, is having a bonfire out at his property. I love hanging out with those boys, but to be honest, a bonfire in August doesn't sound very appealing. Lee-Anne isn't feeling it, either. One of the other options is hanging out at a small get-together at the house of a guy we don't even know. Lee-Anne knows a guy from work who is over there, and my buddy Mike from high school, who I call my cousin, is there also. A few minutes go by with no decision. I'm sipping on my sweet tea, wondering what Lee-Anne wants to do.

Biting on my straw, I ask her, "Do you want to just go over there for a little bit? It doesn't sound too crazy. And I'm still feeling rough. I can't really handle crazy tonight, anyway."

With her tan skin, long brown hair, and big brown eyes, she nods her head and says, "Let's do it."

The verdict is in.

We throw our trash away and hop back in my truck.

The drive to the guy's house is uneventful. We roll the windows down because my AC stopped working earlier this week. My truck, in all of its sexiness, is only three years old. How is the AC already not working? The sun may be on the other side of the world right now, but man, oh, man, tonight's weather is scorching. With the wind blowing through my hair, this hot breeze reminds me of the way I felt about Paul last August. I can't keep thinking like this. I've got to turn my thoughts around. I need to have fun tonight and dance. I want to dance to anything other than his heartbeat.

I really love to back my truck up to park most places I go. This guy's driveway has enough room for me, so that's exactly what I'm doing—backing in. It's so much easier to just pull out when I'm ready to leave. I'm a fan of quick exits.

Lee-Anne and I walk up to the front door, ring the doorbell, and a few guys open it. Two of them I know, and only one of them Lee-Anne knows. They're watching football and offer us a beer as soon as we walk in. They say we are free to grab one out of the fridge. Lee-Anne and I look at each other, and honestly neither one of us is up for drinking tonight. We decline and let them know we just want to keep it low-key and hang out tonight. After going to that club last night, I'd be fine not drinking for another year.

But that isn't the way this party is going to pan out.

After an hour of talking and hanging out, the guys want to play beer pong. This guy named Kevin looks us dead in the eyes and exclaims, "Oh, come on, you guys! You can't leave us hanging! Just play one game. Mike and I against the two ladies."

Ugh. I'm really not in the mood to drink again. It doesn't even sound appealing. But of course, me being me, I turn to Lee-Anne and say, "Haven't you heard before that drinking a beer the next day cures a hangover?"

She chuckles. I really do think I heard that somewhere. Besides, it's just a beer or two. No big deal. Of course, we end up playing more than just one game. Lee-Anne and I dominate one end of the table (I've been known to smash a round or two). Stopping with beer pong would've been good, but now the boys have a beer *bong*. I don't think I've ever done one of those before. Pretty sure I only tried it once for a tiny bit for fun. I know they can get you really messed up though. I don't want to get drunk, so I'm going to tell him I only want a half a beer in mine. That way I can say I did it, but I won't get too torn up from it.

The clock hits 1:15 a.m. and we are having so much fun. My curfew since turning eighteen is one o'clock. Technically, I should've been home fifteen minutes ago, but it's only a twenty-minute drive. Besides, I don't want to leave yet. I feel good. I feel free.

I think I'm just going to sleep here. I'll check with Lee-Anne.

"Hey, do you just want to sleep here tonight?" I say. "I'm supposed to be home already, but I'm not ready to leave yet. Are you?"

"Yeah, let's just stay here. Are your parents cool with that?"

"Well, probably not. I'll just tell them I'm staying at your house."

"Okay," she says. "I already told my parents I'm staying at your house."

I text my mom and ask if it's okay if I crash at Lee-Anne's house. She says that's fine and she will see me in the morning. I know my parents would totally not agree with me staying at the house of a guy they don't know, much less one *I* don't even know. I don't lie to my parents as much as I used to when I was fifteen, sixteen, and seventeen, but I have no problem doing it when I need to. My parents aren't extremely strict, but they are strict enough. Especially when it comes to curfew and needing to know exactly what I'm doing at all times.

People always say parents are only strict because they care, but still, I can't wait to be on my own. Having to check in and always play by somebody else's rules gets old. What I'm feeling has got to be normal for any eighteen-year-old.

Lee-Anne and I are having so much fun at the party. With the different drinking games and all the laughter in between, I can honestly say tonight was much needed. It feels good to escape the annoying routines of life sometimes. And it feels even better to be out of the house and away from the neighbor situation. I can't wait to move on.

Suddenly, though, I'm not okay. I'm walking around, joking and talking like everything is okay, but I'm feeling extremely uncomfortable. I don't know, maybe it's a mixture of the alcohol, the breakup, and being around these guys? I'm not sure. I just don't feel right. Inside I'm sad, yet on the outside I look happy. That's probably the alcohol talking, but I just want to get out of here now. It doesn't feel right sleeping in the same house as these guys. It's confusing to suddenly feel so uncomfortable, but I just don't want to sleep here anymore. I wonder what Lee-Anne is feeling.

"Hey," I say to her, "let's go to the bathroom."

"What's up?" Lee-Anne asks.

We get to the bathroom, and I tell her everything I'm feeling. I also mention to her I want to head out. I want to sleep in my own bed. She's trying to talk me out of it. She's telling me everything I already know. She's saying let's just sleep here and we can leave first thing in the morning. But that's not enough. That's not what I want. I want to go home. I'm burned out, I'm tired, and I want my bed. I want to wake up a new person; I don't want to wake up here.

I'm stubborn. I always have been. If I don't feel right about doing something, I'm not going to do it. I tell Lee-Anne I'm out of here, and she decides to come with me.

We say goodnight to the guys, and my friend Mike tells me to text him when I get home. I giggle and tell him, "Of course. Don't I always?"

We get in my truck. I press down the brake, put my truck into drive, and pull out of the driveway. I have no idea my entire existence is about to change. When I say everything is going to change, I mean *nothing* will ever be the same.

Ever.

7

one choice:
everything changed

I get to the neighborhood exit and make a right.
I have one more left turn before I hit the main road,
and then it's a quick highway trip back to my house.
My windows are down, the sun is long gone, and the
breeze feels so good. I feel better now that I'm on the
road. My mind feels clear, and I can't wait to cuddle
up in my bed with Lee-Anne next to me.

After making a left onto the main road, I pull up
to the light that actually leads to Kristen's house. Her
mom is no doubt asleep right now, and we would have
no problem sneaking into Kristen's bedroom, but she's
with her boyfriend, so we're going to keep heading
back to my house. Damn, I wish Kristen were home.
She's so much closer, and we could just call it a night

there. The light is still red when a car pulls up next to us. It's a red Infiniti, and a man is in it alone. His windows are down like ours. He keeps looking at us. After this light, our two lanes merge into one.

The light turns green, and he speeds up to reach the merge before we do. I'm actually kind of aggravated. Why would he do that? He just cut me off. Maybe he doesn't know I'm a girl who knows how to drive a truck like I mean it, especially when I just want to get home. There was no need for him to pull a rude move on me.

I'm not necessarily tailing him, but I'm probably not the distance I should be. My dad taught me that for every ten miles I'm going, I need to have one car length between me and the car in front of me. That's not the case right now. This guy cut me off. What he did was wrong.

We get a little bit farther up the road. I'm not really familiar with this stretch. I do drive it often, but it's not that close to my stomping grounds. The road isn't drastic or anything, but it does have an S-type bend a little ahead of us, and I'm still stuck behind this idiot.

We reach that slight bend, and this guy hits the brakes. Not just taps them, but actually presses them. There's nobody on the road. Why is he braking? I slam on mine. My truck slides off the road a little, but I correct and get back on. A hundred feet later, my rear right tire catches the shoulder.

Lee-Anne and I look dead in each other's eyes, and then it all goes black.

Everything I say about the accident from this point on has been told to me. I don't remember any of it. I remember heading home, and I remember hitting my brakes, but I don't remember ANYTHING else.

My truck flips around eight times. The guy in the red Infiniti doesn't stop to check on us. He doesn't even call 911. It's 3:25 a.m., and nobody else is on the road. At some point between the first flip and the eighth, Lee-Anne and I both get ejected out of our rolled-down windows. Neither one of us had seat belts on.

The week before, I was annoyed that my windows had stopped working. Turns out, it was a blessing in disguise—getting ejected through open windows instead of breaking through glass.

I fall unconscious immediately after getting ejected. Lee-Anne, however, does not. Less than a mile away, a man named Ed, who has never been awake past nine o'clock in his life is sitting on his front porch. Usually he's up early for work, and so he calls it an early night. But tonight, his son is visiting from out of town. They're hanging out with a friend having a few beers when they hear my truck flipping. All three know exactly what that sound means, and they immediately leave to see if they can help.

When they get to the crash site, this is what they see: My truck is a good distance from the road, lying on its side. Smoke is billowing out of the engine and the tires are spinning. Lee-Anne is lying on her back close by. If the truck had flipped just one more time, she would have been crushed. Although she is conscious, she is completely delusional, mumbling and unaware of what happened or what is going on now. The man's son, Josh, is doing everything he can to keep her calm. She's trying to get up, but Josh is scared and begging her to stay as still as possible. Lee-Anne has no idea what she just lived through.

By the looks of it, I was ejected well before Lee-Anne was, as I am nowhere near her or the truck. I am completely unresponsive. They are trying to figure out if I can breathe or if there are any signs of life. Ed is tickling my feet to see if he can get any response from my body. My legs start moving. He also holds my hand and asks me to squeeze it if I'm okay. I squeeze it . . . having no idea that this will be the last hand I'll ever squeeze.

They call 911. Dispatch answers, and they tell them that they found two girls lying near a truck that looks like it has flipped many times. One girl is delusional, and they're not sure if the other one is going to make it.

When first responders get to the scene, they put Lee-Anne in an ambulance and tell her that she needs to call somebody on the way to the hospital. She decides to call her sister. During the phone call, Lee-Anne keeps saying, "This wasn't supposed to happen, this wasn't supposed to happen."

Lee-Anne also hears the paramedics say that they don't think the other girl is going to make it to the hospital; then she blacks out.

The paramedics want to medevac me. Unfortunately, my vitals are too unstable. So I'm put in another ambulance, and we're headed to the same hospital as Lee-Anne.

My parents get the phone call at 6:30 a.m. Actually, my dad gets the call. He missed the first call because he was in his workout class, but the second time, he answers. On the other end of the line is the chaplain from the hospital.

I'm not a parent. I can't tell you what a phone call like this would feel like. But I do know that no one ever wants to get a call like this. This is by far the worst phone call my parents have ever gotten.

Initially, my dad is told I was involved in a motor-cycle wreck. The chaplain must've said "motor vehicle," but "motorcycle" is what my dad heard. My dad's heart is racing because only the week before, one of my best guy friends, Will, came by with his new street bike. My dad told me I'd better never get on that thing. I never did, but he doesn't know that yet.

The chaplain tells him it is serious. It doesn't look good, and they need to get to the hospital as soon as possible. My dad calls my mom and tells her to drive slowly and meet him there. After arriving, they have to wait about four hours until they can see me because the doctors are putting my neck into traction. This means they are screwing forty pounds of weight into the temples of my head to decompress the weight off my spinal cord with a pulley-like system to hopefully prevent any further damage. Their main goal at this point is to keep me alive for at least twenty-four more hours.

The medical staff are certain of two things: One, I suffered a traumatic brain injury. And two, I broke my neck. My parents have been told only about the neck injury so far and that I'd also fractured my hip.

The doctors aren't sure how severe either injury is yet. The first twenty-four hours are critical after a neck injury. Some people make it, some people don't. They tell my parents that if I can make it through the first twenty-four hours, they will then take me back to surgery and hopefully piece me back together. They can't tell my parents much else until all the procedures are done. For now, the doctors have surgically placed a ventilator into my windpipe through the front of my neck to keep me breathing. This is because, with the severity of my neck break, my respiratory system has shut down. This ventilator, giving me my every breath, is my life support. It's keeping me alive. My body is in and out of respiratory failure. I've been in a coma since getting ejected from the truck.

Everybody is overwhelmed, wondering if I'll make it or not. My family, closest friends, and even Paul have been called. Everybody is told that I wrecked my truck because I was drinking and driving. Paul always told me it was so stupid to get behind the wheel after drinking. He would get so mad at me. He told me to stop. I should've listened.

This wasn't my first time drinking and driving. This could've been my tenth, twentieth—I don't even know. I will soon find out, though, that it was my last, and it's not even by my choice. All it took was once; all it took was one bad decision.

The first twenty-four hours have passed, and I've made it through. I've made it through enough hours now to let neurological surgeons open my neck from front to back to see exactly what damage I've done. I know we have all heard the saying, "Be careful—don't break your neck." Honestly, though, who actually really thinks about what that means? I always thought if you break your neck, you die. Which is about 50 percent true. So, many do, but some don't.

When vertebrae in the neck are broken, there are a few possible outcomes. If the vertebrae alone are fractured or dislocated, but the spinal cord is unharmed, the damage will be minimal. On the contrary, if the spinal cord is affected at the neck level, this can result in full-body paralysis. Death is possible, but it isn't the only option. Those living after a neck injury wake up to the devastating possibility of being trapped in their own body, leaving many survivors wishing that the worst had happened.

When the neurosurgeons are about to take me back for surgery, my mom tells them one very important thing. Between the panic and rush of everything, she says to them, "You let my God work through your hands, and Melissa will be just fine."

The surgery takes four and a half hours. During this time, the prayers do not cease. So many family members and so many people I call friends, even if we've lost contact, are here. Kristen knew she needed to tell my mom about the dream I had, the one about me speaking to high school students about drinking and driving. After she tells my mom, my mom KNOWS there is something so much greater behind this destructive choice I made. She feels that God has not stopped holding on to me.

When the neurosurgeons come out, they meet with my parents. The waiting room is full of family and friends anticipating the news. The surgeon tells my parents he did the best he could, but it's one of the worst injuries he's ever seen. He cut open my neck, both anterior (front) and posterior (back), and pieced together five vertebrae back together with sixteen screws. He fused and bracketed vertebrae C3, 4, 5, 6, and 7. He tells them I have a cervical-level spinal cord injury, and if I make it through, I will require skilled care. If I'm lucky enough to breathe on my own again, I will be paralyzed from the neck down for the rest of my life. The doctors have to be honest about the situation, and my parents can barely digest their words.

Friends and family continue to gather in a circle both outside and inside the waiting room, and they pray for me. A couple times, Aunt Debbie holds Paul's hand while asking God to save my life, and she feels Paul's worry. His hand is shaking as he grips hers.

Everybody will later tell me that Paul was by far the most shaken by my mistake. The number of tears this guy cried aren't even countable. I know that, no matter what happens from this point on, he genuinely cares about me.

Only two visitors at a time are allowed in my hospital room. I'm in ICU trauma on the fourth floor, room number four, and my injury has paralyzed all four limbs. There must be something significant about the number four.

I'm still in a coma and will be for ten days. There's only a single physical scratch on me—a wound on my left elbow from a previous dirt-bike crash that had reopened. But I do have tubes in me everywhere you can imagine: a ventilator, a feeding tube, a pulse oximeter, equipment monitoring my vitals, among others. The internal damage is pretty bad, and when I say pretty bad, I mean really bad. I really hurt myself on this one. My lungs keep failing. They aren't even breathing. Machines are keeping my body from shutting down. Everybody says it looks like I'm just sleeping.

Since the surgery on my neck, I've had no more operations, and if everything goes according to plan, there won't be any more. Only time will tell what the future holds.

My mom and dad are in my room with me. I'm still in a coma; I have yet to speak to them, or even understand what has happened. My mom heads out to the waiting room to switch with Aunt Kimmie, her sister, so she can spend time with me also. As my mom is walking down the hallway, a little lady named Maggie, who cleans the floors, stops her to ask how I am doing.

My mom says, "Her surgery went well, and she is doing just fine. Everything is going to be okay."

My mom starts walking again, but Maggie says, "No, please, listen to me. When I was sixteen years old, I had a car accident, and God saved me." Then she says, "You have nothing to worry about. There are four angels right now working on your daughter. You have nothing to fear."

Again, the number four. My mom immediately turns around and heads back to my room. She wants to see these angels. She's actually expecting to see four big, majestic angels in my room with me.

She gets there, and there's nothing. She sees absolutely nothing. My dad is sitting in the room; my mom tells him what Maggie told her. My dad is a pretty quiet man, but after hearing this, he says, "You have got to be kidding me, Sheri. A gentleman who possibly works here—but I've never seen him before—just left the room and told me the exact same thing."

It's no coincidence. There are four angels working on me at this very moment.

My parents are doing a lot of research on their own. Unfortunately, the medical staff hasn't been very helpful with further care instructions, or to put it in blunter terms, what happens next. They did tell them that a lot of high-level quadriplegics are put into nursing homes to get the care they need. My parents are completely against that. They are determined to find a better alternative. The last thing they want to do, or will do, is put me in a facility instead of back home with them.

My dad carries around a briefcase full of research he's printed out. He's trying to not only better understand what a cervical spinal cord injury is but also help everybody else understand.

As my parents are digging around online, they find one of the top hospitals in the nation for treating spinal cord injuries. It's the Shepherd Center, and it's located in Atlanta, Georgia. The question now is, How do they get me there?

My mom and dad contact the center, and one of their case managers flies out to interview them. They have to answer extensive questions about my injuries. This is because Shepherd's has limited space. One bed happens to be available in their ICU. I don't know it yet, but I am so fortunate to be getting into this hospital and receiving such good care.

Friends have come to visit me religiously. One of my really good friends from high school, Nikki, has even made me CDs of the country music I like, in hopes that I'll hear them in the background and regain consciousness. It seems everybody knows music gets me moving.

My cousin Krista, who I grew up with and who still lives an hour away, has also stuck by my side. It breaks her heart every time she sits next to my hospital bed and sees tears coming down my cheeks. My eyes aren't even open yet, but the tears are running.

It makes everybody wonder if I know what I've done to myself?

8
is this a grown up hospital?

'm being transported today. I'm in an ambulance with my mom and a handful of top-of-the-line medical staff. We're going to the executive airport, where my med flight waits for me.

Our church has picked up the cost for the flight. My parents would never ask anybody for anything, but the pastor and wife of the church heard about my accident and felt compelled to be a vessel.

It's raining, and my dad is meeting us at the airport, but only my mom will be on the flight. The medical staff gets me situated on the plane, and my dad stands outside the airport fence and watches us take off. He's devastated he can't make the trip, too; the feeling in his chest is unlike any he's felt before.

The med flight goes without a hitch, from ICU to ICU. Not long after landing in Atlanta, I regain consciousness for the first time and speak to my mom. It's nothing like waking up in the morning after a night's sleep. I have no idea that anything has even changed. My last conversation with my mom was through text ten days ago, just a couple of hours before the crash.

I'm barely able to speak with the ventilator, but I whisper, "Mom, I feel so stupid."

She is in absolute shock that I have not only been looking around but also said my first few words. She grabs my hand and says, "Why, Melissa?"

"Mom, I feel so stupid. I kept arguing with God."

She's completely taken aback. "What do you mean you argued with God?"

I don't know how to put it into words. I have no idea where I am right now, but I know I don't want to be here.

"I just kept begging Him, 'Please let me go, please let me go. I don't want to live like this.' That's all I kept saying. But He kept saying no, and I just kept arguing. He told me I will live and He will save me. He said I still have many things left to do."

My first set of conscious tears cascade down my cheeks. What am I waking up to? I must have been dying. I must have known I didn't want this life.

My mom is also crying. I want to ask her what happened, but my voice isn't working anymore. I can't get anything else out.

My mom tells everybody about the God conversation. Aunt Kimmie in particular is dying to know what I saw. But I don't know what to say. I don't remember seeing anything or anyone. I do remember, though, feeling every emotion possible, literally all at once. I wasn't just sad, happy, scared, lost, found, or even confused; it was everything . . . all at once. It was honestly the most overwhelming feeling I've ever felt. It's the only thing I remember and the very first thing I tell my mom.

At this point nobody, including her, really understands yet what I've gotten my whole family into, but these first few words of mine give her the peace she needs. She absolutely knows God is still holding on to me. That no matter what happens from here on out, His work is being done. She has felt God's hands around me the entire time.

Later I tell Aunt Kimmie, "I think he was the coolest professor I've ever seen."

She loves that and giggles. I just don't remember if I saw anything or anyone, but I guess I'm not supposed to remember. It must be beyond my human understanding.

It's nothing short of a miracle that the Shepherd Center has only ten ICU beds and the one I need is available. Having my parents' private insurance is the only way I'm able to get into this hospital. If Medicaid had been my primary, the center wouldn't have taken me. But because I'm on my dad's business insurance, I got the last available bed.

Paul is here, and I sing to him, well, really just mouth the lyrics to, Aerosmith's "I Don't Want to Miss a Thing." I can't believe he is here, wherever *here* is. I'm extremely delusional from all the medications I am on, but when Paul stands right next to me, everything feels okay. All I can think about as I'm lying on this skinny twin-sized hospital bed is, How is Paul going to fit into this bed with me?

I want him next to me. There are tubes everywhere, bed rails on both sides of me, and a neck brace keeping my head still; I need more answers.

I ask a male nurse, "Is this a grown-up hospital?"

He says, "Why, yes this is, Miss Melissa. Why do you ask?"

"Well, because if this is a grown-up hospital, I'm going to need a bigger bed. My boyfriend cannot fit into this bed with me."

The nurse and my family chuckle, and he says, "We don't play that game here at Shepherd's."

I don't know why they find this funny. I want Paul to sleep right next to me. I don't like this. I don't like being here.

If you can, put yourself in my shoes for a second. I'm waking up ten days later to a reality I never wanted and never even knew existed. Like I said earlier, I've never heard of someone breaking their neck and living. Of course, much of that can be credited to living in my own selfish world and not really sitting down to hear other people's stories, but I never knew it was possible. Even being raised with two cousins who were born with cerebral palsy, I never knew that one mistake could lead to something so life changing—to something so devastating.

It takes me some time to fully understand what has happened. Since becoming conscious, I've been listening to the story repeated over and over. But it simply does NOT make sense that I can't move or even feel anything below my neck.

I don't remember anything people are telling me. I don't remember wrecking my truck. That night I just wanted to get home. I just wanted to sleep in my own bed. Why didn't I get there?

Doctors, nurses, physical therapists, occupational therapists, speech therapists, family, and friends are all repeating the same thing.

"Melissa, you were drinking and driving. You broke your neck."

"You have a spinal cord injury. You are now a quadriplegic. You won't ever walk again or use your hands. You're paralyzed from your neck down for the rest of your life."

I've never heard of these diagnoses. There's no way this has really happened. I know I'm going to leave this hospital feeling fine. I know everything is going to get better. I'm eighteen years old. I have the rest of my life in front of me. I just graduated from high school, and college is starting next week. What about the classes I've signed up for?

I can't live like this. I don't want to live like this.

Strangers, and even my mom, see me naked now. Privacy has been thrown out the window, like one of my CDs my mom doesn't approve of. Every bit of it is gone. Bathing, dressing, and even bowel care are just a few of the personal things I'm completely dependent on the help of others. That doesn't even include feeding, oral care, every bit of hygiene in general, or even needing something to drink. How do I explain where I have an itch on my face? I can't point, much less scratch it myself. My voice is so low it's even softer than a whisper, and nobody can understand a darn thing I say. These new details of my life make me sick.

"Mom." I'm trying so hard to get her attention, but she's talking to the nurses.

I'm in so much pain. Tears are rolling down my face, I need her to fix my arms. Please look at me, Mom. I'm hurting, I'm hurting so bad. She finally looks and then runs over to my bed. I'm bawling.

"What's wrong, Melissa?" she asks frantically, putting her ear close to my mouth to try to hear me.

I ask her to please get my arms from behind my back. I'm telling her they hurt so bad and are stuck back there. She picks up my limp arms, trying to show me that they are right in front of me. But she doesn't understand; I don't mean those arms.

This isn't the first time I've asked someone to fix this problem. My other arms are stuck, and I just want to scream. We spend twenty minutes trying to make the pain go away. But it's never going to get better. They keep telling me I'm experiencing phantom pain.

Phantom pain is typically associated with people who have lost a limb. Their brain has a disconnect with their spinal cord, and it makes them feel pain in their limb, even though it's missing. In my case, I still have every limb, but because of my spinal-cord injury, I'm mentally feeling a sensation that's physically gone.

Almost every day, we, as a family, or whichever parent is with me at the time, are required to go to classes to learn more about my new situation. I'm calling these courses Screw My New Life 101. Some days I make it to these sessions, but many days I can't shake the dizziness, nausea, and neurological pain. Now that I'm disabled, my blood pressure is extremely low. I wear an abdominal binder and T.E.D. hose (compression stockings) to improve my circulation, but still, I'm miserable. I've never felt so sick in my life. Whenever I have a medical excuse to get out of my required therapy sessions, I use it, and I lie in my tiny hospital bed as still as plywood. I have them wrap a blanket around my head because I have never felt so cold. With my autonomic nervous system shutting down, not only can I not register pain normally, but I also cannot regulate my body temperature.

The body was made to move. The more a human body sits, the more it's at risk for developing problems. I could face numerous health complications now that I'm paralyzed, especially because I'm a high-level quadriplegic.

Here are a few of the complications I'm considered at high risk for:

1.

Blood clotting. Because I can no longer move, I have less-than-optimal circulation, which means my blood can become stagnant, making it prone to clotting.

2.

Pressure sores. I remember the feeling of finally getting to sit down after a long time of standing; it feels so good. But when you sit down, you're still moving your body weight around, without even thinking about it. You adjust. You keep your butt from going numb, your back from getting tight, your arms and legs from falling asleep. How much have you moved around in the last twenty minutes? Since I can no longer adjust my own body, I'm at high risk for my skin to break down and break open. Pressure sores can get infected easily and can even lead to death.

3.

Muscle spasms. My nerves are confused—they keep trying to communicate with my brain, but they're getting disrupted. So instead, they engage and contract my muscles uncontrollably. Muscle spasms can be extremely painful.

4.

Osteoporosis. Since I can't sit upright and put weight on my bones anymore, they're getting weaker by the day; the weaker they get, the more likely I am to get fractures and bone infections. My great-grandma has osteoporosis, for crying out loud!

5.

Urinary tract infections. These are extremely common. A catheter is a foreign object in the body, which can easily lead to infection. Bladder and kidney stones can also form from sediment buildup, and renal failure is common as well—even a known cause of death in quadriplegics. Since I can no longer release my own bladder like I used to, I am dependent on something called a suprapubic catheter. This was surgically inserted into my bladder, straight through the top of my pubic hair line. This catheter must be pulled out and changed once a month, with the goal of preventing these urinary tract infections.

I'm overwhelmed.

My parents rented an apartment while I'm here at Shepherd's. When Paul visits, he stays with them, sometimes for weeks. I wonder how strange all this is for him.

Paul and I haven't talked about it, but I'm assuming we are back together. Or maybe he is just trying to be supportive. Either way, I am going with the flow. He kisses me, and I appreciate every second of it.

With all of this nonsense going on, I wouldn't say I'm a very pleasant person to be around. I am so angry. I still don't understand a lot; I'm not grasping that this is real. I'm mad at everyone around me, but really that's just because I'm so mad at myself.

Today my dad, my brothers, Paul, and I are out-side, gathered around what the Shepherd Center calls the "hope garden." My mom is back at the apart-ment, making sandwiches for lunch. Around us, pet therapy is going on. I guess the dogs are here to give us encouragement. I'm not sure. My older brother has a dog, Duals, but he stays outside. I do think dogs are pretty cool, though.

A lady walks up to me with a golden retriever puppy. I'm not going to lie. This dog is pretty ador-able. But with not having any movement or feeling below my shoulders, I'm not interested in having it sit on my lap. I can't physically move to pet it, and even if it did nuzzle my hand, I wouldn't be able to feel it anyway. I wish they would just leave me alone.

Paul doesn't understand my frustration. He puts the puppy on my lap, takes my right arm, and pets the puppy's back.

"Paul, can you please just stop? This is really stupid." I'm frustrated but only mumbling, trying not to act miserable.

"Well, can you feel anything, Melissa?" Paul says. "Are you trying to pet him?"

I'm so mad. Why is he doing this? I don't want this stupid dog on my lap. I hate this. I hate this so much.

And then it happens.

Out of nowhere, my right arm between my elbow and wrist flips upside down. I cannot believe it! My right arm just MOVED for the first time since the crash! Paul freaks out and asks if that was me. I don't know what to say. I sure hope so! I mean, I *think* that was me. So he tells me to do it again. I can barely do it, but I do it again. That little sucker of a movement is called supination. I officially have gotten my first movement back since arriving here a month ago. I know I'm going to walk out of here. I just know it.

My dad immediately calls my mom. She is so upset she missed it, but she is also over-the-moon excited, and she wishes she were here with me. One muscle has woken back up, and I'm dying to believe this will be the start of something great.

A couple more days pass. They switch out the trach (pronounced "trake") in my throat for another one that supposedly doesn't help me as much. Everything is a process, making me work harder to hopefully get me better. I have returned to a state of infantile dependency, but hey, even infants can breathe on their own. Cue the eye roll. This is bull-shiitake mushrooms.

I am making decent respiratory progress. A couple weeks post injury, I went from ventilator dependent to trach, and now I'm stepping down to a trach that helps me breathe even less. It's been so difficult trying to learn how to breathe again. My dad was trained on how to suction my trach. Basically, he sticks a long straw through the hole in my throat when too much phlegm has built up and my oxygen levels have gotten too low, causing me to choke.

Trach-suctioning is flipping miserable. Once that straw goes through the opening, I only have a second before I start uncontrollably gagging. The way the human body is constructed is unbelievable. But after everything is suctioned out, I feel like I can breathe again, and my oxygen levels are no longer alarming.

Because my level of injury is so high and I've lost respiratory function, it is almost impossible to hear my voice. I have to click my tongue to get somebody's attention, and when I talk, people have to read my lips.

My dad and I want to go outside to get some fresh air, but as soon as I get down the ramp and out in the open, for whatever reason, this air outside does not agree with me. All of a sudden, I can't breathe. And I can't even say anything about it. I'm literally choking. Thank God my dad is so attentive; he sees my head bouncing and my face turning purple. In no time, he's gotten out the suction equipment, and he sticks the straw through the hole in my neck.

What felt like an eternity was in reality no more than maybe ten seconds, and I'm finally able to breathe again. I really don't know when my breathing is going to get better. How the heck do I plan on walking out of Shepherd's if I can't even get my respiratory system working?

The medical staff completes an exam on me to determine where I fall on the ASIA Impairment Scale. They test all my feeling (sensory) and movement (motor), and then they classify me as an ASIA A. Unlike school, an A is the worst grade you can get on this test. It means I have no function whatsoever below my level of injury. I'm a complete C3 quadriplegic.

It's been a full month since the car wreck, but other than the one little muscle in my right arm that has started waking up, nothing else is getting better. This month has been devastating for not only me but everybody I've brought down with me—family, friends, even strangers who have to help me. Between my parents, Aunt Kimmie, Kristen and Lee-Anne taking a trip up here to see me, Paul, my brothers, and other family . . . thank God I've had people with me the whole time.

I keep asking Lee-Anne what she remembers from the night we wrecked. I need to know everything. I need every detail, over and over again. Nothing is sinking in, and nothing is making sense. This is what she tells me:

"Melissa, I remember that guy in the car looking at us. I remember the light turning green and him speeding up to get in front of us before the merge. You were mad he did that. Not too long after that, I remember seeing brake lights, and I remember us turning and looking each other dead in the eyes . . . maybe we knew something was about to happen. I remember an ambulance and all the guys saying they didn't think you were going to make it to the hospital. They didn't think you were going to live. I woke up, and nobody would tell me anything. I woke up in the hospital, and nobody would tell me if you were alive. Nobody. I was so scared. I thought I had lived and you hadn't."

She'd blacked out only once, after the ambulance came. Other than that, her memory prior to the crash is better than mine. I was in a coma for ten days after. Maybe God had to prepare my heart. I don't know if that's really true, because I still feel unprepared. Maybe that's why Krista saw tears rolling down my cheeks when I was still unconscious—I was arguing with God, crying and telling him I didn't want to come back to this. I must've known how difficult it was going to be.

The crash broke Lee-Anne's tailbone and her pelvis. She has to go through a couple months of physical therapy, but thank God she can walk, and thank God she is otherwise physically intact. The butt pain she gets is unbelievable, though. I'll never know how that feels, but I'm certain she must've landed on her butt pretty hard, and I must've landed on my head even harder. I'm thankful it wasn't the other way around. I can't imagine doing this to somebody else. I can't imagine doing any more damage to her.

To top it all off, Aunt Kimmie's husband, Uncle Steve, was diagnosed this month with stage 4 prostate cancer. I don't have personal experience with cancer, but I do know that nothing about cancer is pretty. Come to find out, stage 4 is the last stage of prostate cancer, what they call "terminal." We're not sure exactly what's going to happen, but getting him immediate treatment is imperative. To be honest, everything everybody is telling me, whether it's about my situation, his situation, or about life in general, it all seems like a blur. I hear words, I hear diagnoses, but they're not sinking in. It's not resonating.

Every night after dinner, the nurses put me back in my hospital bed with something called a Hoyer Lift. On the ceiling of my room is a track, and it connects to a net that they put underneath my body. The contraption then lifts me over to my bed (or vice versa, out of bed in the morning). After getting into bed, I have to face every night what I hate the most: bowel care.

You want to talk about privacy being ripped away from you? They perform a routine called "digital hope *love* and me

stimulation." When I first heard those words, both my dad and I thought they were going to be using some type of machine that digitally helped me go to the bathroom. Isn't that what it sounds like? Nope. Instead, they put petroleum jelly on their gloved index finger (which is medically known as your first digit) and stimulate my sphincter muscle by going in a circular motion, which releases my bowels.

What in tarnation? This is one of the most traumatizing things I've ever gone through, and I have to do it every day. I've never in my life heard of somebody having to deal with this extreme nonsense, with nurse after nurse, stranger after stranger, touching parts of my body nobody should even see.

When I'm in bed and the nurse is ready for my bowel care treatment, she first helps me call Paul (if he's not here in Atlanta with me). Tonight, it's going to be a hard call for both of us. He doesn't know it yet, but I'm going to tell him that I think it best that he step out of the picture. I'm honestly not even sure why he's still hanging around after I broke my neck. Don't get me wrong—I am so thankful he has. I love him, and I love having him around. But in my heart, I know the timing is wrong.

Our relationship wasn't working before. How the heck could it work now, if all these medical details we keep getting fed every day are actually true? After a month of being consistently miserable, I cannot be his girlfriend as a quadriplegic, or whatever it is they

92

keep calling me. I have to break up with him. I have to end this before it gets worse.

The phone is up to my ear; it's ringing. Only a couple of rings go by, and he answers. I'm trying to be as gentle as possible. My lungs are still weak, and my voice is the tiniest whisper. I tell him that I love him so much, but I don't think he should keep coming to see me or keep dating me like this.

Paul is crying. It hurts to hurt his feelings as much as I'm hurting my own. I don't want to do this. I feel like I've already lost so much. But at the same time, I'm scared. I'm scared to bring anybody else down with me. I could understand him trying to stick around if we were married or something, but we were only dating, and we were broken up when the accident happened. I don't think it'll be good for him if he stays by my side.

And don't think I don't hate myself for everything I just said and everything I just ended. I used to have it all, and him. But I hate myself, and I can't let that hurt him.

I know our relationship will never fully heal; it will always be scarred, because an accident happened that neither one of us can change. I just hope he never blames himself. This was all my fault. The reality of it is drowning me; Paul has no idea that I'm crying out for help while he is somewhere sound asleep. I should have recognized where my reckless- ness could have, and did, take me. Paul tried to stop me from making bad choices. He tried to make me realize the danger in them. The time spent with him did make me a better person. My mind just never fully absorbed his truths. And because of that, this is the rest of my life.

I spent eighteen years daring someone or something to have the guts to slow me down. Clearly, I lost that bet. I'm screaming in my head, but no one can hear me. I'm drowning in nightmares. Soon, though, I'll realize they're not nightmares. This isn't something I'm going to wake up from. This is the rest of my existence, and because of that, my sky has turned black. There is nothing I can do. I've never heard silence this loud.

It hasn't even been forty-eight hours since Paul and I broke up for what I had thought was the last time, and I feel sick to my stomach. I cave and have the nurse call Paul for me during my next bowel care treatment. I ask him to please keep seeing me like this. To please never stop loving me, even if that means we can't be boyfriend and girlfriend, please just don't leave me like this. Why can't I seem to make up my mind about this guy? All I want is a friend, while I dream of him being more than that.

Well, bowel care is over, and so is the phone call. Paul argued with me. He told me that I had ended things and that he was hurt by it. I think he's trying to avoid coming back into the picture. Not because he doesn't care, but maybe because it's just easier to stay away from it all. He told me I'm not allowed to hurt him again, and if he can, he will come back up to help me get home when I am discharged.

Well, that time has come. The doctor says I'll be discharged in two weeks. I've stopped making progress, and that beautiful thing called insurance has stopped paying.

I keep hearing "We've done all we can do for you."

I want to scream, "What do you mean you've done all you can do for me? NOTHING is better yet!"

Tears are rolling down my cheeks again, I can't go home like this. I can't let people see me like this. There's no way I can be a friend again. Everybody knows what happened; it's not like I tripped and fell. This was not a freak accident; this wasn't out of my control. I drank, and I drove. I did this to myself. I don't want this story. I don't want to be broken the rest of my life.

I thought I was going to be The Miracle. I thought I was going to be one of the few who left this place on two legs again. This isn't how it's supposed to end.

My dad has less than two weeks to get the house how it needs to be. Modifications are imperative. Doorways need to be widened, the shower needs to be made shower-chair accessible, and somehow I need to get up to the house, which right now has only a three-foot-wide walkway and stairs leading up to the entrance. Oh, and there's one more change, and I'm not ready for it.

I have to switch rooms with my parents, since their room is a little bigger than mine and will be easier for me to maneuver. I don't want their room. I want mine. I want things exactly how they used to be. I want to sleep in the bed I never made it back to. I want to be walking on the carpet my feet used to walk on. I'm scared to death of losing anything more than I have already lost.

My truck is totaled and gone. I want to hold on to the few things I have left, but that's not my choice. My aunts Kimmie and Debbie have gone through my room (everything I once called personal) and have boxed everything up and put it in a trailer for me to go through once I'm home and stable.

Yeah right—I'll never be stable.

Thankfully, some people from church have stepped in and helped my dad as much as possible. They're helping him with the renovations, dedicating all their free time to making my home accessible and livable for my current situation. It's more of a tragedy now than when I first woke up from my coma. Back then, nothing felt real. THIS feels real.

Discharging is what the hospital calls "graduation day." I get to leave this place that felt like a prison. But it's not like I get to leave and all of this is over. The real work is only beginning. I've been numbed by painkillers. I'm forced to use a wheelchair. I'm forced to be 100 percent dependent on everyone else. With my level of injury and its severity to the spinal cord,

I have a 1 to 2 percent chance of ever fully recovering. They say that once I'm eighteen months out from the time of my accident, that's all the recovery I'm expected to make. What if I don't recover? What if my body doesn't get any better? I can't do this for the rest of my life. I will end things if that happens.

Now that I'm leaving the hospital, I've also received my wheelchair. I had to go through a whole seating-evaluation process a month ago to find the wheelchair that would fit me best, both physically and emotionally. The truth is, I was sick to my stomach when I entered that room full of wheelchairs lined up against the walls. I was being forced to choose which one I liked, what colors I preferred, and then a specialist would determine what I needed. I was nauseated by it all. I kept telling them I was going to throw up. I blamed it on my injury, the medicine, and anything I could think of, but it was really because I couldn't handle the idea that my legs and arms were being replaced by a wheelchair.

I chose all black. I want nothing other than all-black everything. I don't want to stand out and be colorful or noticed. I want to blend in—and besides, black is the only color I see now, anyway. The fact that I'm getting my wheelchair the day of my discharge is apparently a miracle. I personally don't see anything miraculous about it, but I'm also miserable.

Listen to how amazing this is, though. Remember Kristen, my best friend from all my fun high school days? Well, her mom is a physical therapist and an elderly patient advocate. Part of her work is helping seniors and disabled people get equipment and things they need. Apparently, a lady she was helping had recently passed away, and she was also a quadriplegic. The lady's family no longer needs much of her equipment, including a practically brand-new, wheelchair-accessible Toyota Sienna, a Hoyer Lift like the one in the hospital (except this one is completely automatic), a mattress that actually turns the person lying in it every thirty minutes to avoid things like pressure sores, and a bunch of other unused supplies. And the most humbling part? Kristen's mom mentioned my situation and asked the family if they would sell it all to us. And they said yes! It's a lot of money that my parents shouldn't have to be shelling out because of my stupid mistake, but thankfully they're determined to find a way.

Paul stuck to his word and came back up with my mom for my discharge, and my dad worked up to the last minute with my brothers and our church community to get the house ready. They've put in a lot of hard work. Now my dad has our new handicap-accessible minivan waiting for me outside Shepherd's as I say goodbye to all my nurses, doctors, and therapists. Earlier they threw a graduation party for everybody who was getting discharged. Today's graduating class is me and three other guys.

I don't know about them, but I'm so scared to go home.

Nobody really knew me at Shepherd's. I was just a name on a hospital door. It's scary. I don't get to go home with a cool story like "Hey, world! I didn't quite make it trying to pull off a gnarly stunt, but it's all good!"

Or even a good story like "Don't worry guys! I saved ten kids from getting hit by a bus, and this injury was totally worth it!"

No, not even close. I, Melissa Ann, drank and drove at eighteen. I did this to myself.

We get to the parking garage. Paul is driving my wheelchair with the joystick. A metallic-blue Toyota Sienna minivan sits there, awaiting my arrival. It's missing only one thing: me. Yuck. I've always been a truck person. Trucks just fit my personality and the things I like to do. I never would've thought I'd be the eighteen-year-old who replaced her dead sexy Toyota Tundra with a minivan. I don't want you to think I'm being ungrateful—I'm just bitter. It's not until after I've been forced to go through all these blink-of-an-eye changes that I realize: I hate change. Especially when it's unplanned, unwanted, and (how I really feel) undeserving.

While at Shepherd's, I had to learn about weight shifting. Meaning, since I now have no movement or feeling below my neck, I need to find alternatives to moving the pressure around in my butt and back to prevent pressure sores. A feature on the wheelchair I now call mine is that it helps me "tilt in space." Basically, I have a timer on the back of my headrest that goes off every thirty minutes. When it goes off, I switch the mode in my wheelchair from drive to tilting. The tilting position tilts my chair backward in midair, taking the weight off my butt completely. Think about the last long car ride you went on. What feels better than getting out of your seat, stretching your legs, and wiggling those biscuits? Not much. Paralyzed folk who have more movement than I do can lean from side to side or bend forward to relieve the pressure on their butt. I do plan on getting to that point, but for now I have to rely on this set of very thought-out wheels, which my butt is basically attached to, to relieve the pressure.

Now the question is, How do I press the buttons on my wheelchair if I can't move? Well, I breathe into a straw, and my breaths determine my movement. It's what they call a "sip and puff." The wheelchair I borrowed from the hospital for the last two months operated the same way. I would puff into it to go forward, and every puff after that would make it go faster. I would suck in to stop, breathe lightly to go left, and suck in lightly to go right. Sounds complicated, right? Trust me, I have already had multiple crashes; thankfully, nothing was damaged but I'm telling you, this is so surreal.

I have another straw on my wheelchair that goes into a bottle in my backpack, where I keep water. I really don't fancy water. But after all the classes I was forced to attend where I learned all about my new spinal-cord situation, apparently water is very important, for everyone. It's going to take me a long time to get used to this.

The drive home has been smooth sailing so far. My dad pulls the car over every time my weight-shift reminder beeps. I sit all the way in the back of the minivan, and we don't want to risk someone crashing into the back of the car while I shift weight. Can you imagine? I survive breaking my neck, but then I get crunched on the way home?

The minivan has a rear entry with a ramp that folds down manually, so my dad feels it is safer to pull off the highway. I understand his reasoning, but really, all I want is for this long drive to be over. Thank God I have Paul sitting in front of me.

I'm still barely able to be heard or understood. My loudest voice is a whisper, so I'm clicking my tongue to get Paul's attention. My chest is congested, and I really need help. I hope he hears me.

He looks back and reads my lips.

"I need to cough," I say. "Can you please help me?"

Paul has been so good at working with my disability. He's gentle. And he has done so well with understanding how to help me cough. When my ventilator was taken out, they replaced it with some step-down trachs, and then before my discharge today, they removed the last button. I have been having some serious respiratory issues, though. I don't know why, but I choke a lot, and it's always phlegm. I don't have the lung strength to cough anything up or to stop choking. The hospital taught everybody who was with me this process called "assist coughing." When I start coughing, someone, either my dad or Paul usually, put both their hands on my stomach in a butterfly-like position and push in and up on my diaphragm. It helps tremendously. It literally makes my chest work again.

Being in the Shepherd Center taught us all so much. The staff even sent us home with a big binder full of information about any complications I may have. My dad has labeled it "The Melissa Manual."

The staff also teaches all of their patients how to live in the community again. What I mean by that is, they talk about how I can get used to being around able-bodied people in my new situation—how to interact, how to deal with the stares, how to try to feel normal again. But trust me. Even after the excursions they took me on, there's no such thing as feeling normal when you were walking just two months ago.

For my excursions, I went to a few different restaurants; I also went to the Georgia Aquarium, and I went to the mall, which was by far the worst one of them all. You want to talk about people staring, and in multitudes? That was miserable. I cried with my mom in the public bathroom; all I wanted to do was go back and hide in my hospital room.

I didn't know it at the time, but these excursions actually weren't the hardest part. Now that we're driving home, all I can think about is facing the people I know—having to go out in public and have people ask how I'm doing. Will I be honest? Will I say I'm miserable and hate my life? Or will I lie and say everything is good and I'm happy?

Because I'm falling to pieces.

9
a broken heart, but a fresh start

We turn onto the road our house is on. I feel sick; my stomach is killing me. Well, technically, you could argue that I can't feel my stomach, but I swear I feel every bit of this turmoil. Even though it feels like I haven't been home in forever, I still remember what it feels like to pull into the driveway like it was yesterday.

We park in the driveway (the minivan takes the spot where my truck used to go), and my parents undo the four tie-downs in the car that kept my wheelchair in place; then I breathe into the straw to reverse while my dad guides my chair down the ramp. Not even five minutes later, Paul says that he's going home but he will see me soon.

Although we have been cordial and things have been as good as they could be under the circumstances, I have a feeling he doesn't mean what he just said. Not that he doesn't want to see me . . . something just tells me that, now that we are both back home, he wants to move on. I don't think I'll be able to completely move on, but still, I always assume the worst. I pray he stays at least somewhat nearby while I continue this fight for my life.

I watch him walk across the grass that I walked across the first day I sat next to him in his truck. In my head, I hear the words to "I Need You" by Tim McGraw and Faith Hill.

Since our house is not ground level, my parents found a lift that reminds me of an elevator. The only difference is it's not enclosed like an elevator. It has railings on each side and a flap that raises up and down, depending on what direction the lift is moving. If the lift is bringing me down, the front flap folds down and becomes a ramp; if I'm going up, the flap closes so I cannot roll backward, preventing me from doing any more damage to myself.

I get on the lift for the first time. My dad presses the button to raise it and says, "Welcome home."

I grin and bear it. I go into the house, and everything looks exactly how I left it. As I'm going through the living room into the kitchen, my dad says, "We widened the doors to thirty-six inches so you can make it through better than you would have if we'd left them the same."

I say, "That's probably a good thing." But he didn't understand me, so I say it again.

On the kitchen counter is a really big gift basket Paul's mom sent us. It has a lot of snacks and cute things. That was super thoughtful of her. Now, though, is the moment of truth—the moment I've been dreading. I have to see my new room. I have to go see the change I never wanted.

I wheel around the corner and through the door of my parents' old room. It's practically empty.

It looks exactly how my heart feels.

Back against the one red wall sits my new hospital bed. I wanted a red-and-black-themed room before I broke my neck, so I guess this is my chance to create it. It doesn't help, though, that all I've got to work with is this skinny twin-sized hospital bed that's definitely not sleepover friendly. It's a bed I'll have to be alone in until I can finally sleep in a normal one.

I also have a brand-new big-screen TV mounted on the wall, so now all I have to get is furniture to fill this place. My mom is begging me to make the space feel like a room, to feel like me, whoever this girl is anymore.

Being home is a whole new kind of trying to be strong. Back at the hospital, it was completely different. That place was unfamiliar. I had no memories and no emotional attachments there. I was a name with a room number. But here? Everywhere I look I am reminded of something. Everything I see I feel something. I have this gut-wrenching feeling it's going to hurt extremely bad before it ever gets better.

My mom is a Rotarian in the local Rotary club, and because of her involvement, they have put together a fundraiser for me. The entire town, in fact, is closing down the downtown area and holding this fundraiser for me; they want to raise enough money so my parents can afford all the therapy equipment and supplies I need just to live again.

I don't want to go. I've used every scrap of an excuse I can come up with, but my parents keep telling me I have to be there. They keep saying it is being held for me, and it would be extremely rude of me not to show up. I don't have any more medical excuses to fall back on; I don't know what to do. Why doesn't anybody understand how traumatizing this is? It's not that I feel like I'm too good for this. It's actually quite the opposite. I feel broken. I feel stupid for what I did. I feel like I deserve absolutely no recognition.

It's the big day of the fundraiser, and I'm going, completely against my wishes. Thankfully, at least Kristen and Lee-Anne have come over to help me get dolled up. I'm going to be meeting so many strangers who are donating money to help alleviate this tragedy that was my mistake. Even scarier, I'm going to be seeing friends. Yes, I have missed them, but I'm terrified of what they will think of the new me. I'm hoping everything will feel the same between us.

I'm mad at Paul, and he knows it. He hasn't seen me since we got home. It just blows my mind that he can live next door and not even want to know if I'm all right. Maybe he knows I'm not. And maybe because he knows that, it's easier to just stay out of it. His mom has volunteered to work the silent auction at the fundraiser, and he will be helping her. I don't want to see him. I don't want him to think that just because I am the paralyzed one, I need someone who doesn't want to stick around. But I can't deny it: my heart still wishes that he would stick around and that he would support me and my new disability by standing next to me rather than by helping from a distance.

Kristen is doing my makeup—getting my lashes almost up to my eyebrows—while Lee-Anne is trying to help me get my lady parts back. I was admitted into the hospital at 127 pounds, but I was discharged last week at only 89 pounds. I barely have any fat left, and since I can't contract my muscles either, I've also lost a lot of muscle weight. So, Lee-Anne is trying to give the illusion that I still have a round chest. I guess the fun part about being a girl is that you can always enhance the lady parts with a couple of props. Don't mind me laughing out loud.

Speaking of laughing, I no longer can actually laugh out loud. Not only have I lost the volume in my voice, but I have also lost my laugh. Don't get me wrong—I still laugh. But when I laugh, it is silently—not a single noise comes out of my mouth. All you see is my head bouncing up and down like a bobblehead. It's a little embarrassing because sometimes people don't know what's wrong with me, and they can't tell if I'm laughing or crying! That's another thing on my new To Do list—get to the point where people can understand the words coming out of my mouth and get my loud obnoxious laugh back. But for now, I've got to find that little bit of happiness left in me somewhere and get to this fundraiser. I'm just hoping people show up. I already feel out of place as it is, so showing up to a deserted fundraiser would only make it worse.

I'm in the back of the minivan, my dad is driving, and we're pulling into downtown. I need him to find a parking spot where I'm not visible. With the loudest whisper I can muster, I say, "Dad, can you please park somewhere so people can't see me getting out of the car?"

"Sure, Melissa," he says. Thank God my dad is very understanding of my insecurities.

I just don't know what to expect from this event. From what I can see out the window, a lot of people showed up. I have a fear of someone I know running up to me and giving me a hug and me having no way of hugging back.

My dad helps me down the ramp, and I have one more favor to ask. I click my tongue to get his attention, and he puts his ear close to my mouth.

"Dad, do you think you could please just push me around for a little bit until I get comfortable driving myself around with the straw in front of all these people?"

Keep in mind that this powered wheelchair with me in it weighs more than four hundred pounds. But my dad understands; I know he wants to help me get through this frightening time in my life. I think he's really good at putting himself in my shoes and understanding my thoughts as an insecure eighteen-year-old.

I haven't been at the fundraiser for even five minutes when people start coming up to me, kissing my cheek and telling me that they love me. I've never met many of these people before. Why do they love me? Don't they know what I did to get like this?

Out of nowhere, I see Jack and Judd with a couple other mutual friends! Oh, my gosh! Where do I begin to tell you about these two? I met Jack when I was fifteen years old on a cruise ship with my family. He was by far the funniest person on the boat, just a little lad from England who had recently moved to the States. We connected right away but lost touch after the boat docked and we went our separate ways. It wasn't until a little more than a year later when I met Judd. One night Judd and I were hanging out when he asked me if I wanted to visit his friend Jack, who had just bought a new dirt bike. Did somebody say "dirt bike"? No question in my book. Next thing you know, I was in Judd's passenger seat, ready to meet this guy and his new bike.

We got to Jack's house, I introduced myself, and he said, "Oh, my gosh—Melissa?" Right off the bat, we both remembered each other from the cruise. After reconnecting that night, we've never stopped hanging out since. Between all our wake boarding adventures, days on the lake in his Malibu boat, and him picking me up in his lowered Hummer (with a Gucci interior!), we have had the best times together. He always wanted to be more than friends with me, and no question about it, he is HOT, but you know when you love somebody so much as a best friend, you can't imagine it any other way? It's like that.

"Heyyyyy, guys! So good to see you," I say as loudly as I can with a little smirk on my face.

"Mel, how are you doing? We've missed you so much. Can't wait 'till you get better!"

"I know, right?" I'm anticipating it more than they can even imagine. "What's up with that tank top, Jack?" I say, sticking my tongue out. I always give him a hard time.

He gets all embarrassed and tells me I'll always be the same. I love these guys so much. I wonder if they will ever know how much, or how many memories I have because of them.

My dad is still pushing me around, and I'm being greeted by so many strangers. The outpouring of love is crazy. One sweet woman donated her Volkswagen to be put up for auction. Local bands are playing back-to-back on different stages, and a lot of game-type things are going on, similar to a carnival. My dad is up next in the dunk tank, and I know my family can't wait to throw the ball and watch him fall into the water. It's always the small things that keep us laughing.

I can't even count how many people I have met in the few hours I have been here. I think for sure my face is going to take a week to dry from all the kisses. I can't understand what has people saying they love me no matter what mistake I made. I didn't get the courage to go up to Paul, but I did get the courage to drive my wheelchair independently. I had my dad put the straw up to my mouth, and I took over like I owned this thing. Well, I guess technically I do. It's been a decent night for me. As overwhelmed as I am, I am so grateful for all the support and the generosity.

The amount raised from the fundraiser is unbelievable. Rotary is absolutely awesome. Enough money has been raised to purchase therapy equipment that is close to impossible to afford. We probably would've never even learned about this equipment if I hadn't been admitted to the Shepherd Center. We were able to purchase a standing frame that will hold my body up in a standing position as well as an electrical stimulation arm and leg bike called an RT300. Via electrical stimulation, the bike pedals my legs and arms. The simulation contracts my muscles to work at the time they should be moving based on the pedaling. The goal of this machine is to fight muscle atrophy and osteoporosis, to improve circulation and respiratory strength, and to promote overall optimal health with the long-term goal of possibly reconnecting my spine to my brain. Research hasn't proven yet that anything can cure my injury, but the technology is here, so it's up to me to go after it.

Let me tell you something, though. I'm not motivated, and I don't want to spend my time in physical therapy. I still believe I'm going to get out of this chair regardless, so right now, my focus is on maintaining friendships. That is my ultimate goal. I don't want to be lonely.

Friends stop by and visit while I'm in my wheelchair, or even worse, while I'm in my little hospital bed. I'm constantly fighting feeling dizzy and sick. My dad says I need to drink more water, but I still despise water. He told me I need to get motivated, but I feel like crap. My friends are barely pulling through. Most show up in my driveway when they have nothing else to do.

When they say goodbye, they say they will see me around, but I know that isn't really how things will play out. The "goodbye" part is true; the "see-you-around" part isn't going to happen. I can't just get in my truck and meet up with friends, much less randomly see them around.

I'm trying to find anything that will help me recapture how I used to feel with friends. How do I even be a friend now? To maintain a friendship, or really a relationship of any kind, work is necessary on both ends. But because I now have zero independence, I can't even meet them 5 percent of the way, much less 50, or 100 like I used to. I hate this so much. I miss everything about being the Melissa I was for eighteen years. I miss getting myself out of bed, taking showers by myself, and getting dressed by myself, not to mention feeding myself, brushing my own teeth, or just being able to do whatever I want; I miss it so much. Words can't capture the way I'm feeling or this reality I face every single minute of every single day.

Kristen is three hours south, busy attacking the college life. Kaley is at college two hours north. Sammie is in a new relationship, so I barely ever see her. Paul's visits are extremely few and far between. Thankfully, Lee-Anne comes around quite often. I'm grateful the accident, although horrible, at least brought us even closer. I sit here and think to myself how crazy it is that the crash didn't happen the night before, when Kristen and Lee-Anne were in my truck after an even more extensive night of drinking. I was pretty smashed—we all were. By all accounts, it should've happened that night. All I can think is, Kristen was not supposed to be in that crash. Kristen was not supposed to be a part of what we went through. She wasn't supposed to be in my truck at 3:25 a.m. on August 11—numbers I will never forget.

Lee-Anne and I both survived with different injuries—one walking, one not—but our hearts will forever wear the same scar.

10
a whole new kind of trying to be strong

I rang in the New Year in a way I never wanted to. It's already been close to five months since my mistake left me quadriplegic, and nothing has changed—I am still a quadriplegic. Little by little, my phone has stopped ringing; people have stopped showing up. It's not because I'm a bad person or that they are. It must just be because they don't know how to be my friend anymore. Heck, I don't know how to be a friend anymore. I have nothing to talk about. I bring up the small topics, like "I plan on moving out one day," and "I can't wait 'till I drive again," and "I can't wait 'till we hang out like normal again." At the end of the day, human nature is just pretty selfish. Nobody typically does anything unless it's going to benefit themselves in one way or another. And frankly, nothing about me being a quadriplegic is benefiting anybody else.

I celebrated the New Year out of town with family, all the while wishing I was with Paul. I wish he had given me a New Year's kiss. I miss the feeling of being wanted, but we're headed back home, and I'm begging my parents if I could please go to dinner with Paul tonight. My parents know he's a good driver, so they're letting us borrow the minivan for the night. It's a Friday night. They tell me to have fun and be safe.

My parents are trying to understand for my sake that being eighteen is hard, no matter what. My dad especially gets that I have a lot of growing up to do and that I want to keep my friends around. He told me that if I can respect the workweek and not complain about going to bed at an early time so he can be rested for early mornings at work, the weekends are mine.

I'm in my room, and my mom is doing my makeup for me, trying to get me as cute as possible. She never gets my mascara right. I used to wear a lot. I still want to wear a lot, but no matter how much I say, my makeup just isn't done the way I want it. Little things like this get me angry. Sometimes I tell myself it's just the mascara triggering my anger, but I know that really the mascara is the catalyst for all my pent-up pain. Because my mascara can't be applied right, it reminds me of everything else I can't do myself and how aggravating it is.

Paul is about to pick me up, so I'm trying to calm down and pretend I'm happy.

He helps me get in the minivan, and we head off to dinner. Italian food is the plan, but as we're pulling into the parking lot, it's obvious that the place is extremely busy. People are waiting outside, and the line almost wraps around the building. It's January, it's cold, and I don't want to wait outside. I'm already freezing.

I tell Paul we should go somewhere else.

"So, where do you want to go, Melissa?" I can tell he just wants to eat something immediately.

"I don't care, Paul. You know how cold I get being paralyzed." I say this in my quiet, post-paralyzed voice, but I wish I could yell at him.

What started off as trying to figure out where to eat has escalated into a fight. We pull into the Chick-fil-A parking lot, and Paul goes inside to grab some food. I told him not to get me anything because I'm not hungry. Which is a lie—I'm actually starving. But I really don't want to go through him feeding me right now. I'm over this crap. He's telling me I'm so indecisive and all I ever want to do is argue with him. I keep telling him he doesn't understand what I'm going through and maybe if he would come around more often, he could help me be a better person.

He turns it around on me and makes me feel like I shouldn't expect so much from him right now and that we can't do this anymore. Nothing has changed with us. He's basically telling me, without actually saying it, that he shouldn't have come back into the picture. I don't know why he came back. I do not know how to be a girlfriend. I have yet to be anything he needs or wants.

I couldn't even make it work when I was walking. How in the world could I ever make it work now? This was my argument when I broke up with him over the phone when I was at the Shepherd Center. It's the worst feeling because I'm so much more broken, so much more vulnerable and lonelier than he could ever imagine. He gets to live, he gets to leave his house, and he gets to do what he wants when he wants. I'm left behind. I'm stuck here regardless of what happens between us.

I don't want to lose him or any of my friends. They're all I have. Paul knows this better than the rest of them. I've lost everything, including all of my privacy and all of my self-control. I want to scream at him, Do you understand what it feels like to have nothing, including your own body?

All I can do is cry. There's no screaming. There's no yelling. There's no vocals in my favor. I don't even want to yell anymore. Paul and I have had so many fights, and over the stupidest things. This one isn't really stupid, though. It's just us laying out our future—or actually, the future of us going our separate ways. This mental pain feels like déjà vu. I've been here before, and I don't like it anymore. Sometimes we meet the right people at the wrong time, and sometimes we meet the wrong person at the right time. I'm not sure which one this is, but I'm devastated. I hurt almost as much now as when I woke up for the first time paralyzed.

At least Paul was there when I woke up to this broken body. I don't know what's worse—losing myself or everything I thought I had left.

Paul is heated, so full of anger. I've tried to stop being mad at him for giving up, but I don't know how to. We drive back to the house and pull into the driveway. Then I have to rely on his help to get me out of the van . . . and also to press the button on the lift to get me up to the house. When we used to fight, I would make him pull over his truck, and I would leave. I would find somebody to pick me up and do my own thing. Losing that independence to just be able to walk away or brush it off is something I don't honestly think I'm going to be able to get used to. I don't know how to blow off steam right now or escape this situation.

I get inside, he closes the door, and that's it. It's done—just like that. We've broken up, again. Before, I'd always end up in his bed, trying to fix things. I don't want to go down that road anymore, especially now as a paralyzed woman. I have messed up enough already. The pain used to be intriguing. I could run to it when I wanted to feel it, and I could run from it when I needed to regain a sense of control. But now the running has stopped. It feels like I have a brick wall pressing on top of my body telling me, "I'm sorry, but your time is up."

Paul and I contemplated giving up a while ago; it's time for him to leave and for me to breathe. It's hard losing him, but what has shocked me the most is that I've lost myself, too.

As I watch his truck leave my driveway, my mom walks up next to me.

"Paul didn't want to come in?" she says. "How was it? Did you guys enjoy dinner?"

"It was whatever, Mom. I don't really want to talk about it." I bite the straw to drive my wheelchair; I'm just ready to go to bed and have this day be over.

I'm not trying to be rude, but I am kind of sick of her getting a front-row seat to my circus, knowing everything about my life. I just want to keep some things to myself. I'm not prepared for the "mom talk" about how the right guy is waiting for me out there somewhere. I need that guy *now*. I'm not sure if I can wait, but I'm going to try. I'm making it a goal to wait for whoever he is. I'm saving this body for one last person, and no one else.

I wish I could know right now what my future holds, for better or for worse. In the meantime, all I can do is sleep on my little hospital bed and hope that my dreams are better than my reality.

✳ ✳ ✳

My life currently bites. I'm going to tell you all about it. Dad and Mom have done so dang much; they're currently making so many phone calls to fight for insurance on my behalf. When you go from relying on yourself and your own hands and feet to basically becoming a physical vegetable, you realize there isn't enough help out there for you.

I've been on my parents' private insurance my whole life, but now with this disability, I'm making my way over to Medicaid primary. This is a good thing because Medicaid will pay for the home health care services I need; then my parents can pick up the pieces and start rebuilding our lives. They have created such a beautiful life for us kids, but it wasn't until I went through this life-changing crash that I realized how much of it I'd taken for granted. Including the simple ability to rub my own eye.

It is going to be really different having strangers come to my home and take over what my mom has been doing for me. My dad and brothers also help out where they can. Mom, though, helps me with all my personal care. She gives me showers, she gets me dressed every morning and undressed every night, she brushes my teeth, washes my face, does my hair, as well as any other hygienic/personal care you can think of. She also does my bowel routine every morning at 5 a.m.

It's exhausting for both of us. Not to mention, we have not stopped fighting. I've always loved my mom, but I've never been that close to her. I've never wanted to be this dependent on her. I'm just at that age where we both need our space.

Medicaid couldn't come through any faster; my parents and I need this break from each other. Nothing tests the foundation of a relationship like when one person becomes dependent on the other. I mean, let's be serious. The first hospital I was in, the one before the Shepherd Center, told my parents it would be best for me to be admitted to a nursing home. They said that is what happens to most people in my position. Many families can't stick around. Whether it's because of financial needs or personal reasons, dealing with quadriplegia requires either a lot of money to pay for help or a family willing to sacrifice, well, everything.

My brothers have really stepped up, and I couldn't be more thankful. One is older than I am, and the other five years younger; my accident has impacted them both but in different ways. My older brother and I have always been extremely active, and we like to be daring around each other. My younger brother is only thirteen. He craves my parents' attention as much as I did at that age. I pray he grows up making better choices than I did.

This family of mine is sacrificing everything for me. They refuse to give up on me. My dad has told me he will help me do anything I want to do, including physical therapy at home. He says I *need* to get motivated. Because of the poor economy, his work as an electrical contractor is really suffering right now. And with my mom in real estate, work is either feast or famine for both of them. At the moment, it's famine. I can't fathom what my parents are going through trying to juggle work on top of the repercussions of my poor decision. Like most couples, my parents had dreams. Nothing must feel better than the day all the kids have grown up, and retirement begins.

I am so sorry I've done this to them.

*I just turned 17, landed my first boyfriend,
and swore I had it all figured out
after drinking a few cold ones.*

All I need is the outdoors,
some wheels to ride on, and good
tunes playing in the background.

*This was just a few hours before the crash.
I had no intention of drinking,
but I was around it.*

The exterior damage of my Tundra wasn't bad at all considering what my body went through. The undercarriage though, was considered totaled.

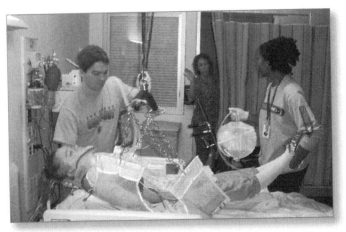

I was in a coma with machines keeping me alive.
I didn't know what I had done to myself yet,
but I was about to be waking up to
a story I never knew existed.

My dad, mom, and family members switched off weeks while staying with me at the Shepherd Center in Atlanta, Georgia. My mom felt God's hands holding me the entire time.

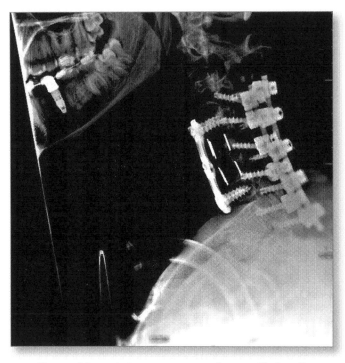

*These 16 metal screws are mine until death
do us part. And even then I don't think
they're going anywhere! Oh, and my
tooth implant is still looking fly-y-y-y.*

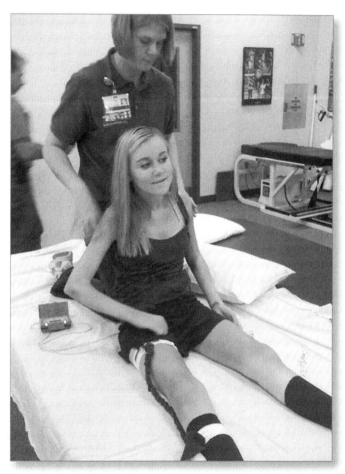

Jayme is the occupational therapist who gave me a new mindset to change my life. I was 89 pounds and experiencing every secondary complication when I first met her.

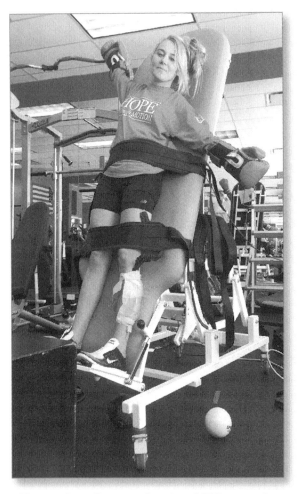

*These days I'm coming in at 115 pounds,
putting in 40 hours of physical therapy a week,
and my mind is healthier than it has ever
been. Oh, you are supposed to punch with
these? Bring it on home—I prefer a hug.*

You can find me somewhere lost in nature with my best friend TobyMac riding on my lap like it is his 9 to 5. Well, because technically, it is.

*A decade into this journey, and I'm thankful
I didn't win that argument I had with God.
Whether this paralyzed thing will last a
lifetime or not, I am here right beside you.*

We both lived with completely different injuries.
But our hearts will forever wear the same scar.

11
i can't do miserable forever

'm so lonely. February has rolled around, and it's no month of love for me. Valentine's Day passes, and so does Paul's birthday the following day. It has taken everything in me to not ask somebody to text him for me. At this point, for me, it would be awkward, so it's just not worth it. In a way, it's like I'm mentally playing with fire.

Life is nothing short of miserable as I sit at home every day watching my ex come and go freely. Not to mention, he is now dating the girl who friends told me he was hanging out with back when we initially broke up right before the accident. Maybe he never actually separated from her, and he just had me believing that things could possibly work between us, even with my paralysis. That makes me so angry. I really do have a lot of anger toward this breakup. I find everything about the ending of our relationship petty. I have nothing but angry thoughts swirling in my head. I see her car parked where mine used to be, and all I can think is, *I hope Paul remembers when the girl next door was the addicting one.*

On a different note, my first home health aide is starting tomorrow. The agency I signed up with thinks she will be a good fit. What does that even mean? Am I getting fit for a life-sized T-shirt? I wish I could say shopping isn't my jam and move on. I don't know what to think about this. I've never experienced home health care before, but I have heard horror stories. I'm hoping at this point I've been through enough and it only gets better from here.

I hope.

Her name is Lynned. She's just a few years older than me and honestly seems like a bundle of fun. We end up getting really close. Not close like best-friend close, but close where she makes me forget my situation. We laugh, a lot. She makes me feel like I used to—carefree, not a worry in the world. She has a six-year-old son, and he is adorable. She explains to me her current situation and how the father couldn't stick around. It breaks my heart to know that a kid is being raised without both parents under the same roof.

Even though my mom and my biological father didn't work out, the man who stepped in and raised me was such a blessing. He took on a commitment he himself was not a part of making, but that didn't matter to him. He cares and that's all that matters. I hope she can find the same for her son.

Lynned jokes around with me after we're done getting through all the chores of daily living. I spend almost every day outside . . . I need nature. When the family of the quadriplegic lady who passed away sold us all her belongings, including the van and mattress I use every day, they also threw in a power wheelchair, even though I already have one. This hilarious home health aide of mine gets in that power wheelchair and joins me, cruising around the driveway and yard. We park at the end of the driveway, in front of the street, and she jumps out of her wheelchair like she is a recovered paralyzed person. I crack up every time. It never gets old.

She helps me forget the friends and ex-boyfriend who couldn't stick around. She helps me forget that my body is no longer working. She helps me escape my reality.

Every night, when I'm stuck in my bed, my brain dredges up every crazy thing I did before my accident—every memory, every fearless stunt. I get so caught up trying to understand why, throughout my whole life, I disregarded common sense and played by no one's rules but my own. I took for granted the independence and freedom I had to escape as I pleased.

What about hiking mountains, running on the beach, or holding somebody's hand again? How can I have a life or do anything? If the rest of my life has to be me in pain, sitting on a wheelchair, making people think I'm happy, I want to check out. I can't do miserable forever. Somebody who is as physically driven as I was should never have to experience not being able to move. I don't know much, but I do know God has picked the wrong chick.

My phone is ringing, and the screen says Kristen! I love getting phone calls from this girl. Lynned helps me answer and puts it on speaker for me.

"Well, hello there, pretty lady," I say, like I always do.

"Oh, my gosh, Melissa. I think I know what you need." She's talking like she can't wait for me to pick up what she's putting down.

"What, a new spinal cord?" I joke.

She laughs and says, "Why don't you get an iPhone like Lee-Anne? They are touchscreen and could be so good for you!"

Hmm. I think for a beat and then say, "I'll have to look into that. Good job, you little scientist, you."

Not even a week later, Kristen's idea leads to a breakthrough. I wheel into AT&T, and I ask them to help me try out an iPhone. They hand me one, and I proceed to type a two-word text message. It's taking me twenty minutes to type two words. I can barely do it, but the point is, I can do it. I have nothing but a little bit of shoulder movement and a tiny bit of bicep, only on my right arm. I setup a payment plan for an iPhone, and I start practicing at home. It is taking forever to type two or three words, but I've got to keep working on this. I need to do something on my own.

✳ ✳ ✳

This is my first birthday with my newly broken body. My parents have a hotel-getaway planned for me with Kristen and Lee-Anne, but something isn't settling right. I don't want to celebrate my life—or any life for that matter. How can there be life when it feels like there is so much death? This isn't me mourning the death of somebody else. This is mourning the death of myself.

My mom and Lynned help me pack my bags. We're going to be gone for only three days, but the amount of stuff I have to travel with as a quadriplegic is unbelievable. It's not just clothes and undergarments. It's bowel care, catheter care, every prescription I'm on . . . and can I even sleep on a normal bed? I've been using an air mattress since the onset of my injury. What about showering? I'm completely dependent on a shower chair with a full backrest for sitting upright. Is the room big enough? There are so many details, but I don't want to make your pretty eyes read every last word.

It's almost time for my big getaway, but first, it's the day of my birthday, and I am on my way to lunch with a sweet lady named Lisa, who stepped into my story right after my injury. Two of her sons are in a youth group I used to attend, and their whole group decided to fundraise for me and my new needs.

My mom and I pull in and park at the hibachi restaurant, and as she is helping me back out of the van, I receive a text from a number I've never seen before.

For a second, I wish it's Paul telling me he got a new number and lost his contacts and that's why I haven't heard from him. Unfortunately, it isn't him. The area code isn't even from around here. The anticipation is absolutely killing me as I'm trying to raise what feels like a super heavy limp arm to unlock the phone. It takes a minute or two, but I manage it and I read the text.

Much to my surprise, it's a happy-birthday message from Lisa's oldest son, the only one I haven't met yet. His name is Jonathan and, turns out, he doesn't live in the state. I'm always down for a new friend, though. We'll see how it goes.

The birthday lunch goes well. Although my mom and I have been having a hard time getting along, I'm really glad she takes me to these lunches. The reason is, I really wouldn't know what to talk about without her. My voice is still extremely weak, so most people still can't hear me, but also, to be completely honest, I have absolutely nothing to talk about. I can only say so much about the few physical-therapy appointments

I go to; other than that, the sad fact is, nothing is changing in my life. I'm slowly shutting down.

Still, though, I'm trying to keep an open mind about my getaway, celebrating my nineteenth birthday with family and a few friends. The hotel is beautiful. It feels like paradise. The rooms and the landscaping make my heart come alive. I'm in the sun, as usual, and I'm watching everybody jump into the pool and splash around. My dad offers to carry me into the pool, but I'm not really up for being held by him in front of everybody. That's just weird. Maybe if I were a kid, I wouldn't care, but not now, not in front of all these people.

Sometimes I don't even realize I'm bothered watching other people be physically active. I have noticed that, instead of always complaining about the same three things, I just tend to get aggravated and take it out on my parents. My mom repeatedly tells me if I keep acting like this, I'm going to push all my friends away. I just tell her I don't care. I get cocky and tell her if I've already lost this much, who cares about a little more? Take it all.

You and I both know that deep down I really do care. Deep down I know I don't have the strength to lose any more. At the same time, though, how does one be somebody people want to be around? You could say I've got a lot of growing to do. I've got a lot to learn.

You'll never guess what Kristen, Lee-Anne, and I decided we needed to get after I was discharged from the hospital. Our first tattoos! They came up with the idea that, since there are three of us, we should each get either "faith," "hope," or "love." I picked "hope." Kristen chose "love," and Lee-Anne wanted "faith." I think our choices couldn't have suited us better.

This birthday weekend means it's tattoo time. I've never gotten a tattoo, before so I don't know what to expect. During the last four months as a pre-paralysis eighteen-year-old, I was obsessed with piercings. I had gotten my nose pierced, my cartilage, my tragus, my anti-tragus, the rook, and I also got the industrial bar in my ear. Who knows when or where I would've stopped? Tattoos are completely different. They're for life. Every piercing I had, the hospital removed before surgery, and the holes are all closed up now.

All I can think is, *I wonder if this will hurt?* I don't have any feeling below my shoulders, but my body still registers pain, just in a different way. I haven't really figured out my new body yet, but I do know that if something hurts and I'm not able to resolve the pain, I will go into what is called autonomic dysreflexia. Due to the disconnect between my brain and my spinal cord, my body still feels the pain; I just cannot send a message of pain to my brain to resolve it. The staff at the Shepherd Center told us that it is absolutely imperative to find out what is causing the pain and fix it. If we don't, it can get as bad as a seizure or stroke. I have already had many ambulance rides to the local hospital to figure out what is wrong with my body.

My blood pressure skyrockets, and I get unbearable migraines, cold sweats, and tingling on my face. Thus far, all my ER visits have strictly been bladder related, so I'm keeping my eyelashes crossed (since my fingers don't work) that nothing bad will happen tonight when I get my tattoo.

Well, I did it. I got a tattoo! Everybody is as shocked as I am that it went so smoothly. I experienced absolutely zero dysreflexia, which is a little bizarre since everyone else who got a tattoo said they felt a little bit of pain. I guess if I can't feel it, I might as well become one big rolling tattoo! One of my cousins, Kahri, tagged along with us and sketched out everybody's tattoos. She is so artistic. My mom decided to get her favorite word, *believe*, on her ankle. I think hers is in the most painful spot out of all of us, right near the bone. I got *hope* on my right wrist, Kristen got *love* on her right hip, and Lee-Anne got *faith* on the back of her neck, memorializing the place I broke. I'm really glad we did this together.

When Paul stepped out of my life, his parents stepped into it. I never was close to them prior to the crash, but now it is so different and lovely. Sometimes when we go on dinner dates, people ask if they're my parents. And let me tell you, they never say that they surely are not. I smirk as they eat up that people think they are my parents. It's always those darn little things in life.

Sharon, his mom, has invited me over to her house to play a game called bunco with all of these elderly ladies. I have never heard of bunco, but I'm accepting the offer in hopes of seeing Paul. His truck is in the driveway when my mom drops me off, and I'm telling you, I have never felt more insecure. Words can't describe what it feels like to date a guy, fall in love, break up with him, and then months later, cross paths after becoming a quadriplegic. What you feel, above all, is left out, in such a heart-wrenching way.

Paul is here, and he keeps coming into the kitchen, which overlooks the living room where I am. I see him look my way many times.

We never speak a word, but it wouldn't surprise me if he heard every thought I had.

Game night is over, and I'm back at home. My dad is about to pick me up and place me on my bed when my iPhone lights up. It's a text from Paul. Oh, my gosh!

He tells me how good he thinks I look. My heart is pounding. It was only two months ago that I figured out how to send my own texts, which in itself is a breakthrough, and now I get a sweet message from Paul. It's not much, granted, but it is a relief to feel something from him again. I feel an ounce of my old confidence bounce back.

On a another note, Jonathan and I are texting pretty often. So many nights before my parents go to bed, they set up the Bluetooth in my ear and click Jonathan's name on my phone to call him. Jonathan and I usually talk for a couple of hours, and when we finally hang up, I just rub my ear on my pillow to get that uncomfortable Bluetooth out. It's worth the minimal ear pain, though. It's nice to have someone to talk to.

He's actually coming down next week to spend the weekend with his family, who live about fifteen minutes from me. I'm extremely nervous, not only because it's my first time meeting him but also because I'm doing my first speaking engagement ever. I will be speaking at my church. I dictated my speech to my aide, and she typed it out, about a page and a half, and I'm going to read straight from it, because I really don't know what else I want to say. I'm not going to lie and say that everything is okay and that I'm extremely happy, so I'm just going to stick with the facts about my injury and keep my feelings out of it. Lee-Anne isn't going to be saying anything, but she is going to be on stage standing next to me, supporting me.

Now that I've been a quadriplegic for these last eight months, I've noticed that, for some reason, people look up to me and call me "an inspiration." They tell me they could never imagine what I'm going through (and trust me, there's no way they could). They also tell me that if I have faith, I will be healed one day. They say it might not be physically, and most importantly, it won't be on my timing but God's, and that Jesus is the healer of all things. I'm told that it's not of

God for us to be broken, and that by giving my life to Him, I just might figure out who I'm supposed to be. Random people come up to me and pray over me and speak healing words. I grew up in a religious family and was taught about God, but now I'm dealing with all these huge physical changes, and it's overwhelming when people continuously feel compelled to come up to me. I feel so much pressure to be some amazing person I'm just not.

What if I don't want to inspire people? Why do I have to be the one to help other people? What about me? Who is going to be my inspiration? Why do I have to be the one who suffers?

Take me from these wheels—I'm aching to be someone new.

My very first, and hopefully only, speaking engagement goes as well as it could have. The love I received from the church members and having little Lee-Anne by my side was humbling. I'm going to be honest. I don't really like public speaking. It scares the mess out of me. I hate talking about my mistake. I want to run away. I want my mistake to pick on someone else while I hide from the world.

Lately, I've been trying to find any way to distract myself. I'm on my electrical stimulation stationary leg bike, and my dad and my aide are with me, as they both helped me get set up for it. I've been on it for only fifteen minutes, but my head is pounding. Something is physically wrong, and we can't figure out what it is.

This is unlike any headache I've had before. One of the autonomic dysreflexia signs I need to look out for is a headache, which I've experienced numerous times from my catheter clogging, but this one is different. This one feels like my head is going to explode. My blood pressure is 180/120. Something is seriously wrong.

My dad unhooks me from the bike, picks me up, and sits me up in my bed. He grabs the "Melissa Manual" we got from the Shepherd Center, and he's rushing through it, trying to find out how to fix whatever is happening. My mom has already dialed 911. I'm crying and complaining.

The ambulance gets to the house, and the first responders load me up as quickly as you can imagine. They don't have extensive knowledge of spinal-cord injuries, but based on my vitals, they know it's urgent. My mom is in the ambulance with me, and my dad is driving separately. Out of nowhere, my left arm starts jumping. It hasn't moved since the accident.

I try to ignore the pain and click my tongue as loudly as I can to get my mom's attention.

"What's wrong, Melissa?" she says, sounding panicky.

"Mom, look at my left arm. Why is it moving?"

I hope I'm not worrying her more, but she turns to the driver and tells him to hurry up.

Then I black out.

I wake up in an unfamiliar room, but with all the familiar medical equipment around me, it must be the hospital. It's a day later, and everybody's telling me I had two seizures. My autonomic dysreflexia got to the point where it forced me into two active seizures. Something was hurting me, and according to the "Melissa Manual," it went unfixed for too long. I already know that I don't drink enough water, and before the autonomic dysreflexia set in, I had a Monster Energy drink. Not to mention I am currently treating a UTI, and I'm on many other medications. Being on the electrical stimulation bike must've set it all off. We're not sure exactly what caused it, but now I have a daily anti-seizure medicine to take. One more pill to add to the cup full of others.

I write on my Facebook wall, "Another hospital visit. I can't wait till my life is normal again."

So many family members come to visit me in the hospital, including Paul's parents and Jonathan's mom. Jonathan's mom even brings me roses; she says they're from Jonathan. All I can do is smile. A couple of days go by, and I'm ready to be discharged. Another hospital visit bites the dust.

12
trying to punch the wind

My day begins at 5 a.m. First my mom gets up, makes her coffee, and comes into my room. My morning alarm is her turning me on my side to do my bowel care. Then comes a home health aide who works from 6 a.m. to 6 p.m.

Medicaid has allowed me to receive twelve hours of help six days a week. The aides do everything for me, and my mom has talked me into starting college. After high school graduation and before the accident, I was signed up for the local community college, but I never got the chance to start. I'm closing in on a year since I broke my dang neck, and my mom keeps saying it's time to move forward.

I've tried pity. It hasn't worked. I've tried anger. That hasn't worked, either. I've tried depression and giving up, but those have brought down not only my world but also everybody in it. So many friends just aren't around anymore, and my family is getting really worn out from all my negativity. I'm thinking it's time to try the one road I haven't attempted yet, and that's forward.

My mom is being the person I don't have the strength to be right now. She's doing everything for me, not just medically but even signing me up for school. She's registered me for one class, psychology, an elective. I need to make sure I can even do this college thing before I sign up for more classes. And quite honestly, I need to ease my way into becoming a student again. I'm not your average student anymore. My arms and hands don't work, so I can't take notes or take a test. I can't flip pages in a book to study. My mom has been in contact with the college's disability office, and it seems like they will provide everything I need. Once I purchase my textbooks, they will get them formatted onto a CD for me so I can digitally read on my laptop. They also will find one student in each of my classes to share his or her notes with me. The cool thing is, the school pays these students for their notes. What college kid isn't looking for some extra cash! Whenever I have a test, I am required to go to the disability office. My professor sends my exam to them, and they provide a scribe to do all of the writing for me. I go into a private testing room so I can verbally dictate my answers to the scribe. I'm already dreading college algebra—that is, if I even decide to get a college degree. How am I going to pass math if I can't even write out the problems? Lord have mercy on my future scrambled-eggs brain.

A paralyzed perk, though, is that I get double the test time, since I'm not able to write out the answers myself. Heck, yeah!

My mom came across something called Vocational Rehabilitation Services, and they will pick up my school cost. The program is funded through the state, and its purpose is to get people of various disabilities back into employment. And cool story moment: they gave me a new laptop, too! Wow, I am so grateful. They installed this program called Dragon NaturallySpeaking. Basically, I wear a headset and train the laptop to recognize my voice; then I can command the laptop verbally. At least, that's the idea. But just like me, this thing ain't perfect. I just told it to go left, and the sucker typed *gorillas*. This is going to take some getting used to.

It's been really fun talking to Jonathan all the time. Just having him show me that maybe I can be loved again is a big deal. I don't know exactly how someone could love me, but maybe it's possible. My heart tingles like crazy when he flies down to visit and we go on dates, and they end with kisses. But then when he flies back home, something doesn't settle right in my heart. I feel like I'm doing something wrong. I'm not sure where this feeling is coming from—other than maybe the Holy Spirit. You know, that gut-wrenching instinct. Jonathan and I aren't even in a relationship. We have just been getting to know each other, but that's enough to make me feel like this isn't right.

Just last night I had to tell him I don't want to talk anymore. I had to tell him I'm just not ready and I'm really sorry but that I am so thankful for the attention and time he has given me.

To make the days a little bit harder, my first home health aide, Lynned, has stopped working with me. There were just a couple of things going wrong throughout the day, and my parents felt like I could get better help. Little did they know, her helping me laugh every day was very significant in motivating me to just get out of bed in the morning. Although, I don't really have a choice anyway; my parents press me to get up and get the day started. They tell me I'm wasting my life every second I choose to not live it. They have always been so active, and so have I.

I just don't know how to be that person anymore. I'm still trying to find the will to live.

I wish Lynned was still my aide. I'm having the worst time. So many strangers are coming in and out of my house, and it's overwhelming trying to teach them everything over and over again. My mom is overwhelmed, too. Every morning, instead of getting her day started, she has to make sure I am properly being taken care of. Most of the time, it's just a mess. Some, and I repeat *some*, of these ladies are even really sweet, but there are language barriers. Most of them have only recently moved here to America and are still trying to learn English. As a quadriplegic, I've learned quickly that there are so many things I have to say.

All I have is my voice. So these language barriers are more than a hindrance; they 100 percent de-motivate me. I just had a girl last week snap her fingers in my face and call me an inappropriate word after I nicely asked her to please wash her hands before applying lotion to my face. This is the kind of stuff I'm forced to be dependent on others for. You have got to be kidding me.

I've been discharged from the physical, occupational, and speech therapy I've been doing since coming home eight months ago. They told me I have made all the recovery I'm going to make and that insurance will not cover anything more. My parents are not happy campers. They were taught very well at the Shepherd Center that my injury is a lot of maintenance. Physical therapy isn't about making me independent again. It's more about keeping me healthy. The goal is to maintain bone density, muscle mass, circulation; to prevent things like pressure sores and bladder infections, which my injury is prone to.

But with insurance refusing to pay for more therapy, what could we do?

Well, getting to know Lisa has been an unexpected blessing. Even though my relationship with her oldest son, Jonathan, didn't work out, her next oldest son is actually dating a girl whose mom is a physical therapist at another hospital. The mom relayed a message to Lisa that a phenomenal occupational therapist is moving close by from the International Center for

Spinal Cord Injuries in Baltimore, Maryland, and this therapist could be exactly what I need, so Lisa referred us to her.

The new therapist's name is Jayme. Insurance approved two-hour therapy visits with her twice a week. I go every Tuesday and Thursday. I don't think she sees my disability when she works with me because she pushes me more than I believe I'm capable of. She is always having me try things able-bodied people can do. I keep saying things like, "You know I'm para-lyzed, right?" or "I don't think this is a good idea," but she has so much more experience and hope than I do. She sees the possibilities and potential progress. She's teaching me to make my injury work for me and to use my muscle spasms to create movement. Even though the spasms are involuntary and completely uncontrollable as of now, she keeps drilling into my head that any movement is better than no movement.

She's a firm believer in a lot of electrical stimula-tion. Since I cannot contract my own muscles, she believes there are many benefits from basically shock-ing muscle groups. And I'm starting to believe her. Even though it doesn't guarantee I'll regain movement, it does create muscle mass, and it fights potential com-plications such as muscle atrophy and even osteoporo-sis, and any kind of movement improves circulation.

Occupational therapy mainly focuses on regaining upper-body movement and function. The goal is to increase independence as much as possible. Jayme has been continuously working on my arms and hands. One day, after doing an arm bike session with the help of Jayme moving my arms for me, I lay out complaints to her for the first time.

"Jayme, I really want to walk again. I've already gotten some shoulder movement back, I can shrug my shoulders now. I'm sure my arms will just get better by themselves. Is there any way we could work more on legs?"

She looks me square in the eye and says, "Okay, I have a question. If you had a choice and you could heal something right now, would you rather have your arms or your legs?"

Without even hesitating, I say, "My legs, of course!"

She smirks and says, "So, say we get your legs working right now. You're going to wake up tomorrow morning, be able to walk right out of bed, and then what?"

I look at her like she should already know the answer. "I'm going to run out of the house and get on my dirt bike again."

Her eyes light up; I can see the wheels turning in her brain. "How? You said you want your legs working . . . so you can get out of bed, but then what? Are you just going to walk around in circles because you can't open the door? And what about clothes? Do you plan on walking through your house, letting everyone see you naked because you can't even get your own clothes on?"

159

I am dumbfounded. How did she even think of that? I would've never thought about it that way. All I want is my legs, my legs, my legs. But she is teaching me that my arms are really what will make me independent. My legs do make things easier, but my arms make things possible.

Jayme is my first seed of hope. She helps me more than she knows. It is so much more than physical. On a physical note, though, she is slowly but surely motivating me to not just work out with her but to also work out at home. I hate knowing I have to dedicate multiple hours a day to work on an injury that isn't even guaranteed to get any better. There is zero comparison between working on a cervical spinal-cord injury and a common injury that can be physically treated, like a broken bone or a strain. I'm not at all saying those injuries aren't difficult, but they have a high probability of healing, or at least coming close to it. Every injury is difficult. But it is different when your whole body shuts down. What I would do for a torn meniscus or fractured arm!

I always wonder why somebody who enjoys TV and sitting around can't face a trial like mine. Why should it be someone who questions what the word *sit* even means? Motocross is life to me. Outdoors and getting dirty is what I do.

Jayme keeps reassuring me, "Melissa, it's more often the active ones who end up getting hurt. But I have met non-active people who have gotten hurt in car wrecks that weren't even their fault, and they were left in the same position as you. It just happens."

I hate that she's right. She tells me time and again that I will find life in a new way. She reassures me that if I dedicate the time for the maintenance my level of injury needs, who's to say what my future holds?

All of these working-out appointments really make me think. I go home, I sit, I cry, and I try to survive. I've put up so many walls and boundaries so nobody can hurt me again, but what I'm realizing is, all that's doing is stopping my current pain from leaving.

I've finally hit my lowest low. I have met depression face to face.

I don't know why God saved my life. I don't know why He kept me in a world that is so physically driven when I have no opportunity to be physical . . . so I can sit trapped in my body for the remainder of this life? That is a cruel existence. People always ask me if I'm angry at God. All I can wonder is, *Why would I be angry at something I can't see, taste, or even sometimes feel?* I'm a very rational thinker, and in my mind, being angry at God is like trying to punch the wind. What is it really going to change or accomplish? Nothing.

He didn't do this to me. I did this to myself. I'm angry at myself. I'm watching friends move out or head off to college. People I know are landing cool jobs and even saving up to purchase a house soon. So now because of one dumb decision, I'll never have the opportunity to scratch my own face again?

I wish I could go back and tell myself that living recklessly does not pay off. I want to throw myself against a wall and say, "Being reckless hurts people" and "You're going to hurt yourself." I wish I was like those teenagers in high school I never hung out with. The ones who knew what was right and what was wrong and didn't have a problem staying away from the things that could hurt them. I don't know why I have this personality. I'm not sure what fuels me to think the way I do and then act on it.

I'm coming up to the one-year mark of my butt being stuck to a power wheelchair, and I can't imagine living another year like this, much less a lifetime. Maybe it's time to end my life. I wish I had never lived to see this.

13

there's one direction
i haven't gone yet

Remember Aunt Kimmie's husband, Uncle Steve? He was diagnosed with stage 4 prostate cancer the month after I was paralyzed. Well, the cancer has been taking its course. It has spread from his prostate to his brain, which is still considered stage 4 because stage 4 is as bad as it can get. He stays at our house often because we have a phenomenal hospital nearby that specializes in cancer treatment. (A month before I broke my neck, their family moved two hours south from us, so it's easier for him to get to all his appointments if he stays at our house.)

For so many years, Uncle Steve has been an employee for my dad's electrical company, and I can't fathom how difficult this cancer diagnosis has been on both him and my dad because he is no longer stable enough to maintain employment. Uncle Steve's situation has been a slight eye-opener for my depression.

Uncle Steve and I try to help each other. He recently had brain surgery to remove the tumors, and it's hurting my heart to watch him slowly decline when he stays at our house. Today, though, has me more heartbroken than usual. I'm in the dining room with my aide; she is working a computer for me, helping me watch YouTube music videos when I hear Uncle Steve dragging his feet behind me, walking to my younger brother's room that we've turned into his guest room. His head is down, and his shoes are untied. I'm frightened something terrible will happen if he trips.

My voice has gotten a tiny bit stronger, so I try and exclaim, "Uncle Steve! Are you nuts? You need to tie your shoes. You're going to trip and fall. Do you want help?"

He barely glances up, his head is still drooping, and he says, "Aunt Kimmie is mad at me again. I messed up my prescriptions. I made her get upset with me."

"Oh, Uncle Steve, let me call her and tell her to lighten up! I'll remind her that she's the love of your life, and hopefully that will make everything all better." I so badly want him to feel okay.

He looks exhausted, but he gives me a little smile. As he's walking away, he says, "Thank you so much, Melissa. You're the best."

I immediately dial Aunt Kimmie's cell phone. She answers, and she sounds flustered. She vents to me that this is not the first time Uncle Steve has messed up his prescriptions. I keep trying to interrupt her and let her know that, Aunt Kimmie, oh my gosh, how precious is this time you guys have left? I fill her in on how sad Uncle Steve is that he upset her and, of course, how much he loves her, and so do I.

We're not sure how much longer Uncle Steve is going to be around, but if what the doctors say is correct, it's not that long. My new situation has made me see some things differently. Before, when I was mobile and distracted by constant busyness, I would've never taken the time to call Aunt Kimmie or even to bother worrying about how Uncle Steve was doing. It makes me sad knowing that all I really did care about back then was myself and how to make my own day better.

It's ironic that I'm grappling with suicidal thoughts and trying to learn how to live again, while Uncle Steve is learning how to die.

It's August 10, the one-year anniversary of the night Lee-Anne and I left my house. Lee-Anne and I decide to go to the scene of the crash for the first time. We're going to drive the same way we attempted to head home and stop to see the side of the road where our bodies landed.

As we're pulling up and seeing where it all happened, nothing is really hitting me or making me feel a certain way. Sometimes I don't even remember I'm in a wheelchair until I see my shadow on the sidewalk. Don't get me wrong: I'm faced with reminders all day every day. But the simple fact that I don't remember anything about the crash, being here feels like a story is being told to me. It feels like someone else's life. It feels like Lee-Anne is just telling me about something that happened to her. This is so insane that we both lived through a deadly crash when so many people don't. I'm trying a little harder every day to figure out the reason behind my second chance.

After visiting the crash site, my family and I go to dinner with Lee-Anne's whole family. My family and hers wanted to get together and celebrate the fact that we're still alive. I cry to Lee-Anne's parents and tell them I am so sorry for what I did to their daughter. I'm so sorry that I hurt her and that I hurt them. They tell me not to apologize. They say my mistake is one that even they have made in the past. The only difference between my mistake and theirs was the outcome. Their words comfort me. They tell me they're so thankful for me and that they can't wait until I can have a sleepover at their house again—although this time without stealing the vodka when they're out of town! We all giggle, and I apologize for that, too.

If someone had to be in my car that night, I am so thankful it was Lee-Anne. This dinner has been enlightening for me. I am now fully aware of how grateful I am that my current situation wasn't swapped with Lee-Anne's. I can't imagine living with myself after doing this to her. I could've killed her; I can't imagine putting her family through that or living with the guilt.

One thing that has helped me distract myself from these "what if" and "why me" thoughts has been college. That one psychology elective I signed up for at the local community college is done. And guess what? I passed with a C! It's a very low C, but can you believe it? I passed! I have an ounce more confidence now that this college and degree-seeking thing just might actually be possible.

Now that summer semester is over, I'm beginning fall semester. I signed up for two classes this time. Just freshman English composition and college algebra. I'll soon find out the answer to my how-to-pass-math-as-a-quadriplegic question. They keep telling me it is just as possible to pass math as psychology. Since college algebra is a required course, I'm going for it.

This semester is much different for me socially. Coming on campus over the summer for one class wasn't hard at all. Honestly, not many students were registered, anyway. But now for fall term? Oh, my gosh, I see so many people I remember from parties, high school, you name it.

Usually, I give a little smirk to invite someone I recognize to come talk to me. But the majority of the time, when they see me and this wheelchair coming their direction, I kid you not, they turn around and head the other direction. Or they just look down, pull out their phone really quickly, and pretend like they don't see me. My heart crumbles every single time. Granted, none of these people were my best friends, but it's normal to just acknowledge somebody you know. The days I have to go to campus, I fall asleep crying at night. Rejection hurts. It hurts really bad.

Once in a while, I catch myself skipping classes to go off and hide in the woods and talk about life with my new aide. Sometimes I feel stupid when I do that because I took all these long public transportation rides to get to class, then I don't even show up. Sounds ridiculous, I know. I'm just having a really hard time right now.

I can't stop thinking about my truck. Those two years, those 80,000 miles I put on it, were my freedom. I wish I had gone on a road trip. I should've made the time to explore past my county's borders. In a way, life is kind of like a road trip. Sometimes people get really far, and sometimes it seems people never even start. So many wrong turns, so many detours, and every so often, slowing down to tune up. Whether it's life or a car, it comes with maintenance. Somehow we all end up where we are supposed to, but first, we must start.

I am constantly trying to act like trying to fit in doesn't bother me, like I'm perfectly fine. But I'm not. Not even close to it. I want to vent, and I want somebody I can relate to, but I can't force either of those.

I can't do this living-in-depression thing anymore. I'm sick of it. I am absolutely sick of it. I want to want to live. I want to wake up and feel like I'm supposed to be here. I'm certain we are not here on this Earth to just feel dragged down. I had an emotional break-down earlier this week when I was by myself outside. I decided to have a conversation with God. Call me crazy, but I did it. I said to Him that I'm so broken. So broken that even "broken" is an understatement. I'm lonelier than I've ever been. I feel hopeless. I hate feeling stuck. I don't understand why everybody else has gotten to move on in life when it feels like I'm sinking in quicksand. I told God, "You know my situation better than even I do." At least that's what everybody keeps telling me. I asked God to please take this brokenness and mold it, to use me. I'm a realist, with a goal of becoming an optimistic one. If I decide to end my life, who's to say that what would happen after is any better than this? I may never understand why I'm still here, but there has got to be a bigger reason. There has got to be something my mind cannot grasp.

I'm hitting a turning point. I'm beginning to understand that as long as you can feel your heart beating, you must have a purpose. You just have to. Regardless of our understanding of the circum-stances, there must be a bigger reason we just cannot understand. I'm starting to realize that if we were meant to understand everything, we would. It's as simple as that.

Sometimes I can't even understand why we humans are the way we are and why we do the things we do—and those ideas are tangible. How in the world could I try to understand a God I don't even know yet?

I'm sick of bringing my family down with me. The economy is hard enough on my parents. They have enough on their plates; they can't carry any more stress. They don't need to keep babysitting me and my future. This is my chance to finally get it right.

I'm counting on this feeling of a new beginning to fill me with reasons to keep on living. Based on my new insights, I am making it a goal to get motivated to do three things. First, school. I don't know yet what I want to major in, but I need to graduate. Nowadays, it's beyond competitive to land a good job. People are getting so much more experience and so many more pieces of paper to their name; the job field is tough. Not to mention, with all my physical limitations, I have extremely limited employment possibilities. No matter how long it takes me, even if I can handle only two classes a semester, I'm going to keep going.

Second, physical therapy. Jayme has been such a motivation for me to not only work toward possible recovery but to also get as functional and healthy as I can with my current level of movement. She has referred me to her old place of work, the International Center for Spinal Cord Injuries. My parents love this idea. I can meet with a doctor who knows extensively about my injury, and I can work with more therapists who care about my recovery as much as Jayme does. Our first trip to the center will be at the beginning of the new year.

Third, and I would say most importantly, I need to spread my message. I need to prevent other people from making the same mistake I did. Every day I wake up to a circumstance that could have been prevented, and I want others to know that. Most people, especially people my age, don't know anyone with a spinal-cord injury, and they almost certainly don't understand the true extent of quadriplegia.

Although my situation is devastating, it has given me the platform to be an inspirational speaker— "the drunk-driver speaker." I'm deciding to own the mistake and accept that it was my choice, and now my consequence. Nobody did this to me, and it's no longer pity I am seeking. I want to help people. I want to be the reason somebody says they made the right choice, or even better, that they never gave up. I just want to use this time God is giving me to be a spark of hope, to help light up this world.

Every day I repeat to myself the words of Isaiah 40:31. My favorite part goes, "For those who wait upon the Lord . . . they will run and not grow weary, they will walk and not be faint."

What if we were built to fall apart so that we could fall back together? I think now is my time to make everything right that went wrong.

Forward—it's gotta be the best direction.

14
positive distractions

"I think you should transfer to the community college closer to the house, Melissa," my mom says from the kitchen. "It can be a fresh start for you."

I'm sitting in the dining room, looking out the window, watching cars drive by. I'm hiding from her because I don't like an audience when I cry. These days, I feel like I'm just always watching life happen rather than actually being a part of it.

It's November, and I'm devastated. Uncle Steve passed away two months ago. Another semester is almost over, and I want to believe things are supposed to end when they do. Things get better, things get worse. My life reflects the way my hairbrush looks after a month's worth of hair finally gets thrown away, and it's more than a good deep conditioning I need.

It's been a difficult journey trying to obtain a higher education, and it's not because of my class-work. It's because, in the midst of it all, I'm trying to be a *person* (not even a better one necessarily). I'm taking only two classes at a time in hopes that I won't overwhelm myself. But you see, going to college is so much more than just passing the classes.

It's devastating being around so many fellow students who can't figure out how to be my friend, or can't even acknowledge me. I've pretended to shake it off and act like I'm okay. I've forgotten there's only a bathroom separating my parents' room from mine, and because of that, they've heard more nights of me crying myself to sleep than I've realized.

"But no matter what, Mom, I can't change being a stupid quadriplegic, and that's why people are scared of me. Sure, I can change colleges, but I can't change my life. I hate myself. I hate being a quadriplegic."

I can't hide my frustration as I watch rain streak down the window. The clouds and I have collaborated too often on being sad. My mom comes to my side and tells me it's going to get better because, according to her, it always does. She tells me to breathe life into every word I say. What she doesn't know is, I'm trying to.

It has been difficult trying to replace my stream of negative thoughts with positive ones. I wake up, and I tell myself I'm going to have a good day, but then the minute I'm dealing with home health aides who couldn't give two craps about me or their job, I'm automatically back to angry. Trust me, I'm not saying it would be any better having only my parents to rely on. I understand that there needs to be separation between relationships and caregiving. It's cumbersome otherwise—on me and the person trying to love me.

The second August 11 rolls around, and I can't for the life of me grasp that I am actually celebrating two whole years of my body being paralyzed. Is this ever going to be over? I say "celebrating" not because I'm overjoyed I can't move. It's a celebration to an extent because I'm still working hard every day, and one thing really has shifted. I'm starting to see God in everything. When I say "everything," I mean *everything*. I don't understand how I didn't notice it before. It must've been all of my distractions. It must've been my tunnel-vision way of living.

I decide to put aside my doubt and take my mom's advice. I'm transferring to the community college west of our house instead of continuing at the one to the east. This college is smaller, and it looks more comfortable. My mom trusts God with every breath she takes. I've tried these last two years to get to her level of freedom. I'm still reaching. I'm still growing. It's a process, and it seems every single one of these darn processes somehow ends up leading to progress. So here I am.

Life, I'm ready to live.

It's my first day on the new campus, and man, oh, man, is it super windy. This campus was built on the top of a hill. I don't like being overheated, but

I'm telling you, the wind is not so much my friend, either. As a quadriplegic, it's impossible to wear my hair down when gusts of wind keep picking on me. Hey, wind, your girl over here is just trying to look cute. Because really, what if my future husband is in one of my classes? I feel like I have my hair in my famous two braids or a messy bun every single day of my life—they're cute hairstyles, sure, but anything repetitive eventually loses its luster.

With that little bit of shoulder and bicep movement in my right arm and due to no other arm movement, my hands have contracted into a loose fist. I'm trying to push these hairs out of my mouth. The more I try, the more I feel like I'm going to wake up tomorrow with bruises all around my mouth. My arm movement is ever so slowly getting better, but its current state has no rhythm. It looks like I'm punching myself in the face. I hope somebody doesn't think I'm over here trying to hurt myself. This could be fun to explain to a worried stranger. The thought puts a mischievous smirk on my face.

Then life cuts me a break. I park my chair in a designated handicap spot inside one of the lecture halls for class, and not even five minutes later, I hear a familiar voice.

"No freaking way! Melissa Ann, what is up? How have you been?"

The last time I saw this tall guy I was still attending the private high school. He's actually a few years younger than me, but the private school kept us all fairly close and tight-knit. Everybody knew everybody.

"Drew!" I am so thankful and relieved to see a familiar face. "I guess that headgear paid off. Your teeth look absolutely amazing!"

We both laugh.

In my later high school years (the beginning of his), he had to wear this headgear that went around his whole face. It basically looked like a circle was strapped to his teeth. I don't know why I think stuff like that is funny, but it's fun now to laugh with him about our younger days. I didn't know how much I needed this laugh.

"Well, I guess it took a wheelchair to slow your hyper self down!" he jokes back.

I laugh and think, *Well, he is absolutely right.*

I've always had so much energy; I just couldn't figure out how to properly make use of it. Instead of changing the world, I just always lived on the edge, thinking that whatever would happen, would happen. And, oh—did it happen. Recklessness didn't pay off for me. I wonder how long it will last for everybody else.

"Oh, trust me, dude," I say, "my life is far from the same. It's nuts what I've dealt with these last two years." I wish that wasn't true, but it is.

He smiles—bright, big, and white—and assures me that I'm too driven to let a stupid wheelchair slow me down. Then he pauses. I can see his mind wandering, eyes darting, trying to figure out what to say next.

"Soooo, exactly how fast does that thing under your butt actually go?" He says it like that's the only thing that matters about my situation.

I laugh. His personality matches his smile.

"I haven't actually clocked it," I tell him. "I'll check it out first thing after classes, but I'm gonna guess a steady six miles per hour, bro!"

He laughs and then introduces me to his girlfriend, who he hopes is the one. I'm certain the rest of the semester is going to be better than the last few I had at the other college. If anything, I have rekindled a friendship, and to be honest, that's all I need right now.

I've lost touch with the people who used to be closest to me. Kristen, Kaley, and Will are off gallivanting around this world, building futures for themselves. Sammie is still five minutes down the road, but a relationship takes up all her time. And even Lee-Anne and I are getting to the point where we aren't seeing each other as much. My heart believes that all of these mates will always cherish me, but I am painfully digesting the fact that everything has a season and reason. Not much lasts forever. We humans are too broken. We are too flawed.

In fact, everybody I've ever known has lost relationships and friendships after high school and college. It happens whenever there's a fork in the road; people choose different paths. I get that. It's just that, all my losses happened just a little bit quicker than other people's. I didn't just lose friendships. I also lost the physical ability to be myself. I didn't just break up with one person, I broke five vertebrae in my neck. My spinal cord and nerves are hurting. My life is crying.

Who hasn't had to deal with changes and with loss? I just can't find any word to describe dealing with the loss of myself other than *different*. I just don't want to see myself that way anymore; all struggle is hard. I've got to stop telling myself that just because other people aren't in my position, they don't have their own grief, too. I need that to resonate in my heart. I'm not a special case.

I don't have any close friends around right now to hang out with. Two years into this new life, and I am used to feeling alone. It's gotten to the point where it's actually comfortable. I don't want to be a burden, and I don't want somebody to feel like they need to lift my burden.

I've been protecting myself, finding comfort in this shell I've created. I stay home because it is easier. I've stopped answering the phone because I am scared of what the person on the other end is going to say or ask. I turn down invitations to go out with new friends and even some old friends. I've stopped running into stores with my mom because I'm scared I'll have to socialize. I hide behind walls because I have forgotten how to interact. I get in my bed many nights before the sun has even disappeared. I shut down way too often.

I've become very comfortable with not living. But my comfort has been at the expense of growing anxiety and depression. Too much time alone can be hurtful instead of helpful—it's been self-destructive for me.

I haven't stopped going to college, but I have stopped trying to be me. I'm tired of people always asking me how I am doing or if things are getting better. It never feels like I have a cool story to tell.

My favorite songs are on repeat. Every day I'm here. I'm healing.

15

a bachelor's degree in hope

So, I did it. I continued going to the community college, and three years from the day I started, my associate's diploma came in the mail. It was amazing reconnecting with Drew. Even people who were uncomfortable at first about approaching me saw me hanging out with him, and they found the courage to talk to me, too. I met some cool people, and my idea of life with a disability slowly began to shift. It didn't just shift in any direction, though. It shifted in a positive one.

I took a year off after getting my associate's before starting my next degree—a bachelor's. I needed time to think. I needed time to figure things out. First, do I want to go through college again? And second, what sort of degree do I actually want? Prior to breaking my neck, I took a test on what job would be a good fit for me, and the results said something along the lines of criminal justice.

During my yearlong sabbatical, I went back and forth with my thoughts. One of those thoughts was, *Hey, criminal justice might actually work.* I mean, think about it. Who would really suspect some blonde little paralyzed girl to have a GLOCK 22 strapped to the underside of her armrest? I joked about this idea so many times with family and friends.

The shift in seeing possibility instead of impairment didn't just happen to me; it happened to everybody in my life. Yeah, it's going to be a long road. And yeah, it's going to involve a lot of help. But who's to say I can't find that help? I started planting the thought in my mind that not only will home health care get better but that also my situation will change if I change the way I think about it. Isn't that the way it goes? Isn't that the magic solution?

This new mindset has paid off more than I can ever put into words.

I can't change what I go through right now, but I can begin to change what my future looks like. We all can.

What started as one class a semester became two. Those two shifted to three, and my very last semester at the university, I was able to take four classes. I wanted to know I could do it. All my friends always took four to five classes a semester, and I wanted to taste that level. I had a goal of not spending another three years finishing up the second half of my "four-year" degree. The cool thing about college is, it goes at your own pace.

I'm a person who's stimulated by growth. If I don't have goals, I go crazy. I need to know I'm working on something, and I need to know I am making progress—or at least reaching for it. In those six years I spent as a college student, I learned so much about life, and I began to see the light again. But that's not because I made so many friends and everybody wanted to know me. I actually didn't have an overwhelming number of friends during college. Although, that's mostly because I lived forty minutes from campus and I couldn't just hop in a car and drive myself places. I just could not have a regular college-student life when I had the help of a caregiver for only very limited amounts of time every day. Two to three days a week, my caregiver drove me to campus, I went to classes, and then we headed back home. I did, though, meet some really amazing people I still talk to. But anytime a degree wraps up, you gain some people, and you lose some people. That seems to be the circle of life.

For me, starting college—putting that first foot forward—was one way I dealt with my grief. I found that sitting at home in bed day after day, stuck on reminiscing about adventures from the past, was not helping me. It was holding me back.

Moving forward distracted me from the things I couldn't change. I couldn't change that my day wasn't going to start unless a girl showed up to her seven-thirty shift on time to get me bathed, dressed, and out of bed.

Instead, I distracted myself in a positive way with school. I didn't enjoy many of my classes, but I went to them. I did what I had to do to pass them. I think we so often have obligations we don't enjoy. But it's neat to think that we even *have* obligations to complain about. And it's enlightening to know that no obligation is permanent.

I majored in human communication. I figured, well, this limp-noodle body can't do much, but my mouth works, so I majored in it! Let me get these vocals going and help people change their lives. I've even toyed with the idea of whether I should get a master's degree. It has its pros and cons. After a lot of thought, and many talks with God, for now I'm going to stop with a bachelor's. God needs me out in our playground, in this uniquely designed, floating-in-the-middle-of-nowhere planet. He doesn't want me in a classroom, consuming my time obtaining a degree that isn't going to make much of a difference with what His plans are for me. That's just my intuition. That's what I believe the Holy Spirit is telling my heart. It could change—life always does. But for now, I'm driven to help people wherever they're at in their journey, going to destinations unknown, as far as my wheels, hope, love, and God plan on taking me.

16
creating rhythm

I have really been enjoying spending time in nature, listening to the birds sing with the summer breeze. Even on this hot day, with all of the humidity, it's been good for me. It's nice having somewhere I can run—I mean, wheel—off to. I'm enjoying you here with me in these words and woods right now.

For whatever silly reason, I've never been a big breakfast person. Some days, I wake up, and I'm absolutely ready for it. Lately I'm falling in love with avocado toast first thing in the morning. But other days, the last thing I want to do is start eating. I feel like my stomach just needs some time to wake up. But boy, oh, boy, come eleven o'clock, I'm ready. And if I don't have a meal in mind, I'm telling you, watch out! Something about lacking nourishment makes me dizzy and changes the way I feel. Someone even came up with a name for it—hangry! (Hungry + angry = hangry.)

It's already thirty-three minutes past eleven now, and my stomach is most definitely talking to me. My ability to eat, even this many years post injury, is fully dependent on someone else preparing my meals. It's not possible for me to eat if someone isn't there cooking and setting it all up for me. I've gotten used to eating out every day for lunch. I do this because it's easier on the people assisting me. And to be brutally honest, not many people have ever even offered to cook for me.

Today, though, is a Saturday. Mom is gone, showing property for her real-estate career, and Dad is cleaning up around the house. I talked him into making me some delicious minestrone soup I've been craving. Through the trees, I hear Dad telling me lunch is almost ready. Off to the kitchen I go!

Dad opens the door, lets me in, and then leads the way to the soup on the stove. We laugh about our weekly visit to get soup when I initially became paralyzed. I would ask him every week, sometimes every other day, to please take me to get soup, salad, and breadsticks. It was a restaurant I was always at before my injury, so I used the place post injury as a way to feel alive. But there's one big difference between then, when I was first paralyzed, and now. Before, Dad would feed me. And the best feeder he was. But today? Dad slides a brace on my hand that will not only keep my wrist stable but also hold on to a utensil. Since I have miraculously regained some shoulder and bicep movements, you better believe this quadriplegic is now independently eating!

"Dad, I think there is a stick or something caught in my left wheel," I say. "It's making a weird noise."

He is now down on the ground like he's changing the oil of his truck, searching for this noise I'm claiming to hear.

"Well, Meliss," he says. "I don't see anything. Are you sure it's wheelie having the problem here?"

I laugh and say, "Yes, Dad, I heard it the whole way up to the house!"

There has always been an immense amount of laughter in my family. Some conversations, though, are much different these days. I talk to my parents about my fear of losing them. I tell Dad I don't want to ever experience that loss. My words can't explain how much they mean to me. I know it's normal to be annoyed with parents when you're growing up, but I wish I had never taken them for granted. They don't have to love me, I know that now. But they choose to. They choose to now be my hands and feet, my hope, and my lifeline.

My mom and dad dated back in high school. They were too young then for their relationship to work out, but life had a funny way of reconnecting them years later. They both got married to other people, they each had a kid, got divorced, and then reconnected with each other. So this father of mine may not have been part of my procreation, but he sure did take my mother and me as a package deal when I was just one year old. He cracks me up when he says he was framed! Haha!

These parents I get to call mine have given up their life for me. I'm addicted to their love. I wish I could pray to never lose them, but I know that is unrealistic. So instead, I'm thanking God for these moments I get to spend with them. I haven't met my husband yet, but I'm telling you, he's got to be one darn good man to take me away from these two. There are no replacements for family, distant or immediate.

Dad and I are still hanging out as I eat my soup. We've got '80s hair-band music blasting, and my dad is cracking me up with his quiet yet clever humor. Out of the corner of my eye, I swear I see his hand shaking as he's moving something from one counter to another.

"Is your hand shaking, Dad?" I ask, almost missing my mouth with the spoon.

"No, you silly goose," he says while cleaning up the minimal mess he made. "I'm no shaker!"

"You and Mom can't get old, dude. What are you gonna do if you start getting the shakes?"

"Well," he says, "I guess I'm going to have to get a microphone stand!"

"What the heck! A microphone stand?" I have never heard this man sing in my life. What is he talking about?

He says, "For if I need to use the bathroom!"

I'm laughing hysterically. "Are you referring to a hotdog on a microphone stand?!"

"You know your mother thinks it's bad enough if I don't lift the toilet seat!" He can barely get the words out between his booming laugh. "So I'm thinking for the sake of my marriage, it might be best to invest in a microphone stand to keep things like a horse, you know, *stable!*"

My head is bobbling like crazy from my mute laughter. This is the funniest thing I've heard all day. Where in the world does he come up with this stuff? That was the best lunch I've had in a while, and it's not even the soup I'm referring to. Thank you, God, for making this guy my dad.

I heard yesterday that a friend of a friend was on vacation last weekend with his wife and daughter. While at dinner, his wife started complaining she was dizzy and her head hurt in a way it never had before. So off to the hospital they went. A bunch of tests later and they find out she has a brain aneurysm (a weak blood vessel in the brain that balloons and fills with blood; it's extremely rare: less than 200,000 US cases per year). By then, his wife was on life support. But not for long. The following day, she died.

This wife and mother (among so many other titles) was on vacation when she was taken somewhere none of us here on Earth know about yet.

My throat feels like it's closing up whenever I think about how fragile this life is. Death is inevitable—we know this—but, somehow, it never gets easier to understand. There's so much we don't, and won't, know right now. We do know, though, that on any given day, it could be one of us. It's hard, but I need to focus on giving to those around me, on just living to love them and appreciate them, because none of us knows what might come next.

We will never have all the answers for as long as we have left to live. I'm throwing in the towel on that one. Man has tried to come up with every way imaginable to make sense of this world we wake up to every day. And yet, there is still only faith to rely on.

I'm on a remarkable journey, and I have the goal of overcoming my weaknesses a little more every day. I want to make this world an ounce of a better place. I want to inspire people to get through every day not so much focused on how they're feeling but on the fact that they're still alive to be dealing with it. Let's be less human and more being. And now, if you'll join me, I have a date back outside!

It is a toasty summer day. This girl is taking her wheels to a shady spot on our two acres. My parents have lived here since I was fifteen, and I hope they stay here forever. At twenty-eight years old, I still love this place. I always wonder where I'm headed to next. Shoot, I have no idea, but I think it would be very cool to live on wheels the rest of my life. I'm not referring to my wheelchair, you silly goose! I would love to live in an RV—then home is where I park it. Travel the country and help as many people as possible. Where can I sign up?

I find it exhilarating to not know where life is headed and to have to wait on answers, even though waiting can sometimes be exhausting—am I right?

Time and experience have shown me that if I look past my human blinders and try to think more like God, waiting is actually not wasting. On the contrary, waiting is working harder than I could ever imagine possible. That makes sense too, because isn't waiting itself hard work? Oh, my gosh, I think all the time that if I could just keep constantly moving forward, that would be so easy—there'd be no waiting necessary. But then I wonder, where would the challenge in that be?

I need challenges to accelerate. Sometimes I need forced change in order to change. I get too comfortable. I become too complacent. I forget what it feels like to grow. But I know we need each other; I need you, and you need me. I can't sit here and tell you that I want to love myself again, because I don't know if I ever did. In the past, I unknowingly used distractions to replace the emptiness inside of me. I used alcohol, parties, a boyfriend, daring friends, and a V-8 Tundra to just go. To just run. To just escape. That's what I did, and that's how I chose to manage.

Throughout these bittersweet years since my paralysis, I've wondered, Why me? Why did it have to be me, when every single person I used to associate with did the same things I did? I was never a bad person. I, just like so many others, sometimes got caught up in making careless choices. So many other teenagers have made the same decision to drink and drive as I did, but they never had to face a trial like the one I still wake up to. So many others have yet to be touched by tragedy, when I feel like I am sometimes drowning in it.

I was so miserable when I first became a quadriplegic. Being surrounded both physically and mentally by memories of my previous life—the ones I'd never get back—left me gasping for breath. Even to this day, I'm still on a journey, trying to get better every second I get to breathe. I'm nowhere near perfect, and I never will be; no one will. I don't ever want to look at somebody and think I have chosen better things than they have. I have a benefit or two, and I have a flaw or a few. And that's neat, because everybody does. It's too perfect how we humans can fit and work together, even with all our differences.

Differences. Accepting them is something I'm continuously working on. I have had to rely on more home health aides than I can count on both my fingers and toes, and probably yours, too—heck, probably even five times that. Man, it has been rough, but here's a cool story moment:

Three years post injury, I was forced to celebrate my twenty-first birthday living in a nursing home. Unlike most newly minted twenty-one-year-olds, I wasn't out taking birthday shots; I was literally getting shots in my arm to prevent infection. Let's put it this way: nursing homes don't have the cleanest history.

What a transition it was.

Every day of the week prior to leaving my parents' home (my childhood home), I jammed out to Billy Joel's "Movin' Out." The lyrics hit home more than ever because, in order for me to move up, I really did have to move out.

To cut a long explanation short, my insurance changed from Medicaid to Medicare primary. Because of that, I lost the twelve hours of home health aide services I had received since the onset of my injury. I could never get all twelve hours back, but there was one way to get back at least nine. But to get them, I had to live in a nursing home first, to prove that I do not have the level of care from my family that I need and therefore need the state to pay to get some sort of services in my home care.

My biggest concern moving into a nursing home, though, was, Does this place have room service? Food delivered bedside? Why not! Well, turns out nursing home food doesn't even come close to the good home cooking I'm used to. But I found at least one silver lining to all this mess. Yeah, the nursing-home situation stinks really bad, *but* what have I been talking about since getting discharged from the Shepherd Center? I've been nonstop telling friends that one day I'll move out. My accident happened right after high school graduation, so I've had to watch all my friends leave their parents' care and begin experiencing life as an adult. Me? Obviously I didn't realize how impossible true independence would be for me in my new situation; I've reverted to toddler status since the crash. Well . . . here you go, kid, be careful what you ask for. You've moved out.

My mom came every morning to assist with bowel care and to make sure I slept okay. My dad came every night to get me ready for bed (not the undressing part! Eek! I've got no time for funny business, having my father see me naked! A CNA at the nursing home does that, but my dad put all the stuff I sleep with at night on my body for me). My brothers showed up when they could between school and work. A few friends even came by. How many people can say their roommate was ninety-eight years old? It was very interesting, and I found perks the whole way through.

And you want to know the coolest part? Not only has it given me a whole new perspective on what being grateful really means, but it has also helped me realize how much worse life could always be. If I didn't have my parents, the level of care I need would leave me in a state-run nursing home. I can't imagine spending the rest of my existence in a place like that. My family is still my everything. My dad is such a team player—the way he loves and motivates us kids to grow. My brothers keep me laughing. My mom is still my advocate, the one fighting for so many of my services. She is the brains and has done extensive research on how to better my situation.

Luckily, in the end, I had to be in the nursing home for only three months. That was hard enough, but at least it gave me a chance to view life a wee bit differently. And it gave me the chance to thank God before life got any harder. I'm home for good, and that thought has never been so liberating.

Since the accident, I've drilled into my mind that I need to thank God for *everything*. It's too easy for me, and maybe even others, to almost expect that things should work out and go according to how we plan them. Every day when my aide starts up my handicap-modified vehicle, I thank God the engine turned. Living in a stable country, having everything we could want accessible almost everywhere, can very easily leave us expecting life to end up a certain way. No doubt I lived that way, too. I would start up my truck because I expected it to start. I would go get my hair retouched with highlights and pay whatever price because I had the money—because I'd worked for it. I never stopped and said, "Wow, thank you, God, for allowing me to drive to work. Thank you for giving me work. And thank you for giving me extra money to spend on things such as hair appointments." None of those are a given. Yes, they're a product of hard work, but never a given. I have found it's safest to never expect but to still be surprised by everything. Because who doesn't love surprises! I roll through every day now wondering what it will bring, what will be around the next corner, and I'm always thankful for even the slightest blessing.

That, my friend, has been my way of living. I haven't recovered. I'm not healed yet, but I'm content. Isn't that all a human could want?

In the past, I saw caregivers helping only elderly people. I can't say I recall ever meeting a girl in her twenties dependent on the help of strangers. Because of that, my mental adjustment to this situation has taken more years than I want to admit. It is extremely difficult to rely on stranger after stranger, being forced to depend on them and trust them with every aspect of your life. Your home is supposed to be your safe place. It's supposed to be where you feel the most you. It's supposed to be your comfort zone. I had to realize that if I wanted to maintain relationships with my family, I needed to let these caregivers be my everything. I needed to give my family the time they needed for themselves.

For years, I couldn't find an ounce of peace in home healthcare. The situation itself is extremely difficult for the caregiver and the one being cared for. There is minimal growth in home care. What I mean is, there are no healthcare benefits for the employee, much less any raises or incentives to do their job long-term. So, here I am, trying to love people like God loves me. He gave me many peaceful years of home healthcare with a few different girls who were super close to my age; they came in and gave me so much of their time.

It's hard losing people. I know my time with each aide is limited, but my heart still breaks every single time I lose one. It burns deep down, especially since I recently lost the aide who has given me the most time—an amazing three years. But still, I'm not bitter. On the contrary, I am so grateful for every one of these girls who has fallen in love with my story and given me her time. Of course, I'm still human; I still struggle with the loss. The human in me wants to curse, wants to scream, wants to fight the air around me. But because I have felt years of peace with home healthcare, I'm realizing an angry heart isn't going to change anything. I'm trusting in a deeper way than ever before. I'm looking at aides and not automatically thinking, *Well, gosh, let's see what could be wrong with this one.* I'm finding the things each of them does best. And I may not be getting as much done in a day, but I'm getting out of bed, and I'm living life anyway.

After the nursing home adventure, I was placed on a state waiver that gave me back those nine hours of help. I also have a case manager for my waiver, and she has to visit me every month to ensure that my living conditions are stable with the help. My case manager is here now, and for the first time since knowing me for years, she sees me cry. She sees me gasp for breath as my mom wipes my tears for me. I apologize and tell her I've been holding these tears in for too long. I confess I'm simply overwhelmed with losing caregivers, and I just don't understand why these aides cannot get paid more money—so they want to stay, so they want to help me live my life. She walks me through the whole government-funding talk, and she motivates me to not only learn as much about it as I can but to also maybe even try lobbying for the disabled.

I keep repeating to myself, "I don't know. I don't know if I can do it. I want to be a voice for the voiceless. I want to be the hope for the hopeless. I think I have some work to do."

I woke up this morning at 4:30 a.m., two hours before bowel care. As I lay there staring at the ceiling, all I could think about was wanting to go for a run to kill time, or at least be able to transfer myself into a manual chair and push it down a trail until my arms stopped working. Right then, by myself so early in the morning and unable to move, it hit me how truly weird it is to have a body but only be able to feel your head. But then I realized, I quite possibly have the best seat in the house. I get to step into the future with hope, I get to look for the brokenhearted and reach out to others.

Lying there, I couldn't stop thanking God for how far things have come, and how far they are going.

There aren't always right answers and perfect solutions for everything and everybody. I learn, and I break. And then I begin to see the light through the cracks. I'm a hardheaded son (wait, daughter?) of a gun. I see what I like and build or burn bridges to get it. That's it. That's my personality. I'm driven, and I thank God I'm letting Him be the one to drive me now. It has been ten insane years since I broke my neck, and I haven't looked back since.

No, really. My head can't turn that far anymore.

17
a wild ride

My driveway is lined with trees, and my beautiful vehicle is one of a few parked on it. I still have that same handicap-modified Toyota Sienna. It has more than 250,000 miles on it, and it looks a bit tired, but that's because we've shared so many adventures together. Where do I begin to tell you all of the life this van has given me? I'm thinking four years post injury would be a good place to start . . .

"Oh, my gosh, Kaley, get in your lane. Slow down!"

I'm screaming from the back of my minivan (because I can do that now—scream, that is). My voice has gotten louder over the past few years, and you better believe I love using it! Kaley, my dear friend—how do I begin to tell you how much she means to me?

We're coming to the end of another year, and I have finally been discharged from occupational and physical therapy for the second time. I'm not dropping out of therapy completely, though. I'm just dropping down to forty hours a year. I'll use those hours for visits to the International Center for Spinal Cord Injuries in Baltimore, Maryland. But in my hometown, therapy is wrapping up. It's devastating because I've gotten very used to my routine. I've also become very comfortable with all my appointments. One thing I asked God the year I finally got motivated was to please never let me lose my therapy. Thank goodness He has stepped in. I still use all the therapy equipment I got from the town fundraiser, and we have also come across another therapy center. This one is a little different though. Insurance does not pay for it. Thankfully, this therapy center has a foundation, which has picked up the majority of my therapy cost. What happens when that runs out? Well, that's also in God's hands.

I called Kaley the other day and told her the sadness I'm carrying from losing these therapy appointments. I told her this will mean three days a week I won't know what to do with my time. I told her that I didn't want change anymore, I'm doing so well. It's been almost two years since I've seen a hospital room. I don't miss the medical days at all.

Well, what did Kaley say? She said she was coming over in a couple days. A couple days have passed and she did come over, and now we are on our way to Jo-Ann Fabric. Kaley drives crazy! I honestly don't know how she hasn't totaled five hundred cars by now. Somehow, though, she manages to keep the car upright. I'm barely managing in the back, but I am laughing.

She brought over to my house every kind of art supply she owns; she wants me to learn how to paint. I keep telling her I don't think I have any creativity. I mean, I know I have *some*. I used to make a lot of scrapbooks, and sometimes I would even draw. But paint? I'm not so sure about this.

"Melissa," she says, "painting is not that difficult. Honestly, if you make a mistake, you can cover it up. And if you want to know the truth, nobody knows it's a mistake anyway. They only know what you tell them. That's what art is. It's supposed to be fun. It's supposed to be messy."

"I know, Kay," I say as the automatic doors to Jo-Ann's open and let us in. "I just am not able to draw, or even lay anything out on a canvas to begin to paint. All I see is limitations. I'm not seeing any possibility with this one."

"Well, Melissa, you told me you lost therapy. Don't you think doing something is better than nothing? You're already doing as much as you can in your work-out room. Why not try something new? If it doesn't work, we'll stop."

That's all I needed to hear. I just don't want to feel limited. I don't want to feel like I have to do something when my mind is telling me I'm not able to perform. Since I can't cross my fingers, I'm crossing my eyelashes and hoping this is not another thing that ends up on the laundry list of stuff I can't do.

We find a 16x20 canvas and a cupcake-painting guide that Kaley can trace for me on to the canvas. I think I'm going to give this first painting to our mutual best friend, Kristen.

"One problem," I say to Kaley. We're at the check-out counter, and she is taking my wallet out of my backpack while the cashier is staring at us.

I always have the urge to say to these starers, "Yes, I'm paralyzed. Yes, my arms don't work, either." They always look so confused. But I have been told firsthand numerous times that I don't "look disabled." Whatever that means. Although, I guess that's a good thing because that was my first goal. I didn't want to look atrophied.

But the staring still hurts my feelings, and sometimes I just wish people would use their voices instead of their eyes.

"What, Meliss?" Kaley drags out the "s." She's probably wondering what qualm I could possibly have now.

"Well, I don't think TobyMac is going to be very happy if he can't stay on my lap. You and I both know how addicted he is."

TobyMac is my ten-pound buddy. We got him just two months ago. He is half shih tzu and half something else. We don't know his full doggy ancestry, but he's basically love. He was a rescue puppy we found online, and at this point, I can't imagine life without him. He's roughly nine months old and extremely attached to sitting on my lap. Even when I'm not in my wheelchair, he is right next to or on it. Something about my disability makes him feel safe.

"Looks like you will just have to tell him things are going to be a little different today," Kaley says with a smirk on her face.

Somehow we make it safely back to my house. Usually my day consists of at least three hours in my workout room. Today, though, things are most definitely different. Painting is just as difficult as I imagined it would be, and I'm spending the whole day working on this first masterpiece.

Kaley has done about 65 percent of the work. I'm scared to mess up, so any fine lines are done by her. She sketches out what I'm supposed to paint, and I do my best to make it happen. I can't promise perfection, but I am trying. My shoulder, where my feeling starts, is on fire. This is a workout I need.

Last week, I woke up missing the feeling of *really* being talked to. I woke up and I thought, *What am I doing? I want to feel alive again.*

So this is my year of starting to live again, and the cool stories have already started creating themselves. Life is like that. When you're out and about, memories are made. Even on days you don't have spectacular plans, life happens, and so often you go to bed with a smile on your face. The weeks have become months, and the months have become years. As the time has accumulated, I have started to have more nights with a dry pillow. I am seeing hope everywhere. I'm starting to become it.

Even though I've never seen my life as inspirational, other people have. Now I realize, sometimes it takes adversity to bring light into dark places, and that's what I want—to be a candle in a dark room. The coolest part about candles is, their light can be passed along. My light could ignite somebody else's, and who knows how far that could go on? So now, this is who I am. This is what my heart wants to do.

I'm reading and learning how to push down pessimistic thoughts and doubts, to crush them with every turn of my wheelchair. I tell the evil in this world it's not welcome here. I speak life, and I tell the darkness to get away from me. The internal battle is always raging. There is no permanent up or down. Instead, every time I feel down, I know have to find a way back up. Finding new things to wake up for has helped. There's room here for only one thing, and that is love. No doubt it's time to be Rubbermaid and bounce back!

After my life was saved, I had the same two choices everybody has: to fight or flight. And let me tell you, I am so happy I chose not to give up. I'm just trying my best to live my best life. Choosing happiness has felt like the more difficult route, though. It is just one foot forward over and over. It is so hard to pick myself back up and begin again. It is absolutely draining. But every time I do, I'm noticing it slowly gets better. It may take months, or it may take years, I may be in my chair forever, but one thing I never want to worry about again is choosing to fight. Once you choose it, I think it chooses you. Every sunrise I wake up and whisper to myself,

"Whatever you do in this crazy life, don't you ever stop trying. Don't you ever stop waking up when the sun does."

A few months have gone by since my first painting adventure, and it was nothing short of a refresher. Kaley has come over every Wednesday without fail. I recently have started painting without her. I've gotten to the point where I want to do it by myself. I feel like I've had a lot of practice, and now it's time for me to show off everything she has taught me. My first solo painting is one for my mom, of course. I'm painting two wineglasses in between a bottle labeled Vino. Why, you might ask? Because she loves her red wine, and I love her. So this one is for you, Mom.

It is still strictly bicep and shoulder muscles that make this possible. I'm able to hold on to the paintbrush with no finger function because an aide puts a wrist brace on my hand. My feeling still stops where my shoulder begins, so I cannot take my eyes off what I'm doing. Otherwise, who knows what the heck would be going on? The pain I feel throughout my neck and shoulders after a few hours is intense. It's weird to describe. It's unlike anything I ever felt when I could walk.

Tapping into my artistic side has been nothing short of a blessing. It helps me feel free. It's encouraging to focus on something I am ABLE to do. It's a blank canvas every time. Because of the progress I have made, the first four years led me to acceptance.

Throughout this time, I told myself that I would recover after four years. Something about the number four felt promising. All four limbs were paralyzed, I was on the fourth floor in the fourth room at the hospital, and according to their cleaning lady Maggie, there were four angels working on me. And because I believed in that number four, I put life on hold, just waiting for my miraculous recovery.

The mind is so powerful—most of my limitations have been self-made. I'm recognizing this now, so just a week ago I made a plan with my cousin Krista. Not just any kind of plan, but something I've never done before. I'm going to go on a lengthy road trip. My first road trip without my parents. I'm nervous. I'm feeling hesitant, and I'm wondering if I should bail. I don't even know if I should've agreed to this. It's just that there are so many details that go into me leaving home. What about bowel care and showers? What if I wake up in the middle of the night? Or what if something goes wrong? I'm comfortable with my parents. They know my injury as well as I do. Many times when I ask for things, it doesn't even feel like I'm asking because they already know what I need; I feel like I'm less work around them. I worry I'm going to be a burden on this trip.

I call Krista for reassurance. We decide I should bring my current home health aide, who has been with me for a year. I am comfortable with her, and I'm comfortable with Krista. Krista also says she is bringing a friend, so I think the group will be a good mix.

It's time. Time for my first big outing. I'm nervous, but also excited. I have felt like a toddler for quite some time with my situation. Sometimes it's been disheartening, trying to relearn the fine motor skills of a three-year-old, relearning how to feed myself, and getting my voice loud enough to be heard and understood. But this? Leaving the care of my parents for the first time in more than four years? What words can describe how I'm feeling? None, none at all.

My aide, Fabienne, and I are waiting in the drive-way with our suitcases next to us. Krista's black Nissan pulls in, and it feels like my heart's jumping out of my body. This is a rush. I have that anticipation you get right before you whoosh down the biggest drop on a roller coaster.

Going on vacation also means I actually get to sleep in. Usually the bowel-care nurse comes in at 6:30, but this time? It's just me and these cool people—no invasive alarm!

We've been on the road for about three hours. The friend Krista brought is some guy I've never met. I know Krista really well, and I also know every person she has been friends with, but nothing about this guy looks familiar. He is covered in tattoos and has huge gauged ear piercings. Okay. I'm determined to find out who this guy is.

"So how do you guys know each other?" I ask Krista from the back of the van.

Krista and this guy turn and look at each other, and then she starts laughing loudly. What's so funny?

"We don't," Krista says, still laughing.

Wait, *what?*

Fabienne turns around and looks at me, her eyes wide.

"What do you mean, you don't?" I say with disbelief.

"We just met this morning," Krista says.

"WHAT? You're telling me I'm leaving the state with a complete stranger?"

This can't be true. No way.

Krista and I go back and forth on this for ten minutes, but Fabienne and I still don't believe her. You see, we're going to Atlanta, Georgia, to attend the concert of a band Krista loves, and apparently, she went on the band's Facebook page to see if she had any mutual friends who also liked them. This guy Chris was the only one with similar interests. Krista messaged him the other day, asking him if he wanted to join us. So he and Krista aren't complete strangers.

They know people who know each other, but they don't know anything about one another.

"Aren't you the one, Melissa, always telling me to live life and come out of my shell?" Krista says.

She is right about that. I've always told her life is so much better when you get out and experience it. I am a break-the-barriers enthusiast. I'm not a fan of confinement. You can only imagine how much it's taken for me to get used to relying on other people and a power wheelchair.

"Well, yes, of course," I say. "But I didn't think that would mean three females would get in a car with a male stranger one day! And when I say three, remember one of us is completely paralyzed!"

Krista and I are still so different, even after my accident. Back in my walking days, I was the fearless, let's-do-anything person. Krista, on the other hand, suffers from more anxiety than I do. This used to separate us back in my able-bodied days, but now that I've had to slow down, I've learned how to get to know people for who they really are. Her heart is huge, bigger than mine ever has been. She cares on a deeper level. That's probably why she has even done home healthcare for years. She helps people get what they need rather than focusing on what they have done.

That's an especially beautiful thing for me, because it wasn't something pretty that landed me in my predicament. I can say from personal experience how wonderful it is to meet people who can see past the faults.

Krista is one of them, so I'm going to trust her on this one.

18
my mess becomes
a message

My first road trip was a success. Not only did I go to a concert that had a homemade elevator made out of plywood and chains, but I also felt freedom the way it was intended to be felt. Krista brought me to the hospital in Atlanta that taught me how to live as a quadriplegic, the Shepherd Center. It was liberating going back to the hospital that saved my life. That's when I found out that Chris, the guy Krista brought along, had a quadriplegic mother. She has passed away, but no joke, her name was also Melissa. And even crazier? His birthday is the date of my crash, August 11. My name is tattooed across his chest in remembrance of his mom. I am shocked. It's so insane that we cross paths with the right people at all the right times. Divine appointments much?

To this day, I can now say I have been on multiple road trips since that first one—not only with Krista but also Kaley and Will. I'm slowly breaking away from my mindset that I'm "too much work."

Sometimes you come across people who love you no matter what.

I've also become friends with multiple paralyzed people. Side note: I used to wheel away from these folks as quickly as possible. The idea of being friends with them freaked me out. With all the negativity I was drowning myself in, I didn't want to also be around somebody else's. And for whatever reason, seeing the differences in our abilities brought me down, especially if they had fewer limitations than I did. But now? I'm embracing their friendship with everything I have. Truth be told, everybody needs themselves a paralyzed friend or two. I'm just saying. Are you mentally prepared for some mind-boggling stories? Sit back while I tell you how some of these fellow-injured folks became quadriplegics.

One girl was on vacation in Key West with her family. She had been diving in a lagoon all day, and she wanted to take one last dive before heading in (having no idea she was going to break her neck and this would be the last dive of her life). No one in her group knew the tide had gone up and down instead of the normal in and out, so she dove in headfirst, hit the bottom, and now she is considered a low-level quadriplegic.

A guy I recently met was lying on his hammock one evening after a long day at work. He had a beer or two, dozed off, and flipped off his hammock. He landed on his head and broke his neck. What the heck!

And just when you think you've heard it all, one of my newfound best friends was on her bicycle riding to work. She pulled up to a trolley-car train track and looked both ways. She saw a train coming from one direction, but she had no idea that another trolley train was hidden behind the first one and was also moving in her direction. After the first train passed, she started heading across the tracks, collided with the hidden six-car trolley train, flew off her bike, and broke her neck.

What in absolute tarnation?

These accidents were pretty much out of their control. Can you say God had a different plan for them, or what? But the majority of spinal-cord injuries are alcohol related. Drinking and driving is one, but water injuries are common, too—diving drunk into oceans, lakes, and even pools. When a state of mind is altered, so are future choices. Why not make positive choices *now* that benefit the rest of your life?

Putting the future aside for a moment, today is such a busy day for me. I just wrapped up independently eating another lunch, and now I'm headed to a few speaking engagements. A few years after my injury, when my emotional healing began, I started contacting organizations. I also contacted high schools and anybody else who had ears to hear. I knew God had given me a story to tell, and I am driven to tell it.

Sharing my story publicly puts me at the risk of other people's negativity. It's a hard place to find rest in, but I couldn't live with myself if somebody ended up in my position because I chose not to share my story somewhere. I carry this weight because every stranger means something to me. Just the other day I was leaving an ice cream shop because nothing felt better than a kid's cup of chocolate. Not to mention, it was hot as coconuts outside. The person I was with was further behind me as they were throwing away our trash. Well, I guess when I rode by two ladies walking, one of them asked the other if she knew why I was in my situation. My friend overheard the other lady responded with, "She decided to drink and drive and paralyzed herself." I guess you could say it pierces a new part of me when I hear those words leave someone else's lips. Can you imagine if each of us had to wear a sign around our neck that said how many times we drove after drinking? People wouldn't be as quick to judge somebody else's circumstances if everything they've ever done was laid out on a table for anybody to see. It's hard to live with the goal of helping people, but it also is absolutely worth it.

I am partnered with Mothers Against Drunk Driving (MADD) as well as a few safety councils to be a motivational speaker. Between the two, I speak to nearly seven groups of DUI offenders every month. I also reach out on my own to speak at high schools, middle schools, alternative schools, juvenile detention centers, and even county jails. I tailor my message to each audience, but, for the most part, I keep many details the same. And the one thing I always bring to every engagement is passion.

Even though I'm dedicated to what I do, I still have mental battles between passion and doubt. That little word, *doubt*, has crept into my mind numerous times, often making me discredit myself. In the past, my doubts have told me my story is boring, and they have even said sharing my story isn't effective and I should stop. On the nights when I can't fall asleep, I pour my heart out to God. One night in particular I was talking to Him, and I felt something almost like a silent scream pierce my conscience. Loud and clear, God told me that it's not about me anymore. I have lived enough years selfishly. My story is for His children. I need to help every person I possibly can. I need to use every bit of time and talent He has given me. My job here is to populate heaven. My other job is to be a hope dealer.

Today I spoke at the local detention center to three different groups of juveniles. This place is one of the hardest for me to speak at. I had a very stable upbringing, which I am extremely thankful for, but so many kids at places like this come from unstable homes. I have heard firsthand from them that sometimes their families have even encouraged them to make poor choices.

Now I am wrapping up a DUI speaking engagement with a sad heart. Hearing these people's stories break me. But I know it's healing when people have somebody to talk to, so I listen.

After I speak for about twenty to thirty minutes, the facilitators of these classes require an interactive portion. Most people are not comfortable speaking in front of everybody, and trust me when I say I understand the feeling. One man is telling me in front of the class that this is his third DUI. He says, "I'm not proud. I spent fifty-six days in jail, and I lost my license for five years. I deserve it."

"But no," I respond. "You don't deserve it. None of us deserve pain. We make terrible mistakes, too often again and again, but don't think you deserve hurt. You deserve life. You deserve grace. It's always been right here. Sometimes our minds look past it as we're only looking at ourselves. Don't you know it's so much more than you and me. It's so much more than us."

A smirk of disbelief flits across his face and cuts through his tears. He's hurting, and I can feel his cry for help.

Another guy, younger than myself, tells me he was drinking one night and tried to be responsible by sleeping in his car, in the backseat, in a parking lot.

He says, "Did you know you can still get a DUI just by being in, on, or near a vehicle with the keys in the ignition or even just near you? As long as there is accessibility for you to drive after drinking, you are fully capable of getting a full-blown DUI, and I repeat, that's driver's seat or not."

I knew this, but so many others in the room are shocked. I love it when someone else steps in and shares new information.

He continues, "There's no such thing allowed as sleeping in your car while intoxicated. A .05 percent blood alcohol level, which for most body types is typically just one drink, gives you tunnel vision. Only .05 percent alcohol in your body turns off your peripheral vision."

So many again are shocked. This guy is speaking the truth. I can tell that his experience has transformed him—I hear it, and I remember it. My goal isn't to stop people from drinking. My goal is to show people that it's safer to accept our own limits and weaknesses. Multiple other people in the group tell me they have stopped drinking because they do not make good choices when alcohol is in their system. I always tell them that it's not a matter of how much they drink that determines if they have a drinking problem. It's too easy to rationalize, to tell yourself, "I only have a beer a day—I'm not an alcoholic." I tell them the only way to know if they have a problem is to look at what they do after they start drinking. If what they do doesn't involve smart choices, it might be time to evaluate drinking, and maybe stop. Alcohol is a very effective dissolving agent. It dissolves our bank accounts, it dissolves our relationships, it dissolves our professional life, it even dissolves our insides. But the one thing it never dissolves is our problems.

My goal is to inspire people to have a good time responsibly. We've all made a mistake here or there—some of us have just had to face the consequences quicker than others. I always leave a reminder to never judge somebody based on their circumstances.

I'm praying for the opportunity to speak at every high school in the nation. Prevention is key. And I'm telling you, I am at this country's disposal. Pave the way and, by golly, I will be there.

My time at this DUI meeting has come to an end, and I am leaving the class with my little dog full of love, TobyMac, on my lap. As I'm navigating through the doorway, I remind the class, "Aren't we all just pieces looking for where we fit? You never know the hurt or heart someone has behind the face you see. Please promise yourself to never give up. The dream is free, but the hustle is sold separately. I love you guys. And I can't wait to see just how far this life takes you."

It has been a draining day, but I'm grateful for it. I try my best to let everybody know that as long as their heart is beating, it has a purpose. I can't tell anybody what their purpose is—that's a personal journey—but, oh, how I wish I could. I'm just certain that we all have a purpose in this life, and it is not to hurt ourselves or anybody else.

19
a soft heart

life during my teenage years was all about chasing my dreams. I wanted my future to be life on my own. I struck out. I was just a young girl—just a baby. It hits me so hard sometimes that my future was completely messed up by my own choices. It actually breaks me. I thank God for my home health aides, the good ones, who have stepped into my life. The one who brought me to my speaking engagements today is taking me home now.

I have only forty-five minutes until Kristen gets to the house. We are headed to dinner tonight to catch up on life. When we were teenagers, we said we would meet up in random countries between all the busyness of our adult lives. Not a complete spoiler, but it didn't exactly end up that way. Kristen now lives in

Australia, and I've been here, working and waiting for her return.

On the drive home, my caregiver tells me she thinks my speech was very effective today. That warms my heart. You see, this caregiver, Alicia, is a quiet one. I stare out the window and thank God for the girls who have remained in my life.

There was a little bit of traffic on the way home. Kristen beat me to the house by only a minute or two. She's waiting by her car, and as soon as I roll out of my van, she screams and hugs me harder than I was prepared for. I love these moments. After a kiss on the cheek, she tells me, "You have no idea how much I have missed you, pumpkin head!"

We get to my room, and she helps me freshen up. It's after 4:30, so Alicia has left. It was a day well spent, but I am really looking forward to this friend-time. I tell my parents we will be back soon, and Kristen and I drive off in the van.

We haven't been on the road for even five minutes when Kristen says from the driver's seat, "If you don't mind, Melissa, I have so many questions for you."

I tell her, "Trust me, I am an open book. You are more than welcome to ask me anything you like. You know, even with my limitations these days, I will give you the best of me."

I love food of all ethnic groups. I am American born, Irish by blood. To me, genetics are simply just genetics. I don't think they accurately portray who a person is. Maybe we chose our life in heaven; maybe it was given to us. I don't know the details. But I do love people who come from one race—the human race.

We park in the designated handicap spot at our favorite hibachi restaurant. Kristen and I both love foods of all sorts, and we especially love all the herbs and flavors we can get, so in that sense, we're a lot alike. The owner of the restaurant greets us and tells us it has been way too long since he has seen our pretty faces. I blush and wheel to the side of the hibachi table we usually sit at. It's difficult not being able to fit underneath the average table with a power chair, but thankfully, I travel with a lap tray. So on this beautiful night, it's just Kristen, me, and anything she has on her mind.

We sit, well, technically she does, and her eyes are practically giving away everything she is wondering.

"Are you sure you don't mind all of my questions?" she asks, her eyebrows raised.

"Kristen! If you don't stop questioning life, I will find a way to get you in a headlock." I smile at her to let her know it really is okay.

A tear rolls down her face, and she says, "I just can't understand how it's already been ten years."

Oh, no. I don't want to cry tonight. My eyes water, but I'm holding back the tears. The only problem is, my heart has become so soft now that I feel pain way too easily. This decade has taught me many, many things. With all of the people who have stepped out of my story, I now know it's important to put myself in other people's shoes. I'm telling you, if paralysis had happened to one of my friends, or even ex-boyfriend, I don't know if I ever would have showed up. I don't know if I ever would have been the somebody they needed. I've had anger in my heart for far too long. Not necessarily directed at anyone in particular, but always at myself.

"You know, Kristen," I say, "it blows my mind. So often I roll through the motions. I find it easier to focus on the obligations I create for myself. I mean, don't you? Don't we all? You know I have a good balance between work and play. I'm at this point right now where I'm begging God to keep using me. I was broken. I feel like every day I'm getting molded. I'm ready for His story in my life to explode."

Our stories are different. Kristen is an established woman now. She moved to Australia after falling in love, and my heart sings for her. She's a full-time employee working at a big event-planning company. She travels the world organizing venues, big and small. She loves it. I think our mutual desire to travel and have big experiences has always kept our relationship strong. But even with this strong foundation, things between us have still changed. Not for any other reason, though, than the fact that life changes after high school.

After I broke my neck, Kristen went to a university south of me, and that put some major distance between us. Plus, I'm sure it was hard for her to figure out how to be my friend again. I'm telling you, I had no idea how to be her friend, or anybody else's for that matter. Before, I had always been the one to round everybody up and get something going, but after the accident, I didn't have that fire in me anymore.

Kristen wipes away her soft tears. Her heart is good. It always has been toward me.

"Do you think one day everything is going to start working again? It's just hard that I knew you so well before, and now I'm trying to understand what it feels like to be going through your situation. I can't relate even if I wanted to. I just want to know things will get better again." Her hazel eyes are brimming with hope.

"I wish I had a definite answer," I say. "I wish I had a definite timeline. I wish I knew if I was still waiting to wake up from a nightmare. I think all the time, What if walking was the dream? What if that's when I finally woke up and met reality, when my body stopped working? Sometimes I feel like this isn't even real. I love my parents. I love the life I have created for myself. But I also know there's so much more for me. Maybe it's just my heart dreaming louder than the reality around me. I just have this deep-rooted feeling that this isn't the rest of my life."

Both of our eyes flood with tears. It's enlightening to spew some reassurance. It's nice to know people haven't completely let go.

"Well, I couldn't agree more, Melissa," Kristen says. I can tell she's relieved. "I know you're not supposed to be sitting forever. Maybe your life is just kind of backwards. Maybe you're spending the younger years paralyzed, and you'll be in the Olympics by the time you're sixty." She chuckles. "But no, really, you'd better be carrying me across the finish line!"

My laugh is still silent, but my head is bobbing, and I feel like every tooth is showing. "Of course," I say. "Who else would I be carrying? I'll have you under one arm and TobyMac running right beside me for the first time!"

The funny moments keep us going. Life has too many letdowns, sometimes too much negativity. I enjoy people who are full of life and always striving for more. I know Kristen and I will be friends for the rest of our lives. Even if we're thousands and thousands of miles apart. I am certain life will continue to allow us to meet up. I choose to believe that it is in our favor to cross paths.

"What do you miss the most, Melissa?"

Ah. Where do I begin? I could tell her it's the independence, the simple things like getting out of bed, showering, getting myself dressed, and leaving whenever I want to. I took all of that for granted before. I never thought of them as fortunate. But I want to say more than that. I want Kristen to really feel what I am saying. I think for a moment and then say,

"You know those nights when you can't sleep, or the ones when you wake up for no reason? I miss wrapping my blanket around my body, dragging my feet to the fridge, and looking for something, ANYTHING to eat. I miss the privacy of going to the bathroom. I'm sick of a stranger having to touch my private areas for me to go. I'm sick of my parents pulling out my suprapubic catheter every month to avoid infection. It's painful, Kristen. I fight the secondary complications of paralysis with all of my physical therapy, but don't you know I can't wait to just live again? I will always be physically active, but I can't wait for the reason to be more than just hoping to stay out of the hospital. And you know what else? I want somebody to try and love me. I'm sick of my power wheelchair scaring everybody off. People look at paralyzed folk as completely asexual. They look at us and instead of fearlessly approaching and asking us how we manage, all they can think about is how much must be wrong. I see it in so many eyes. And it breaks my heart; sometimes my heart doesn't even feel like it's beating anymore."

I know I'm off on a tangent, but venting helps lift the weight off my shoulders. I hold a lot inside. I'm just over the way people look at the wheelchair community. Sure, some of us were born like this, and some of us were injured during the course of life, but I don't think anybody would choose this life. Nobody wants to be looked at differently. It hurts. It aches in a crowded room.

I continue, "I want people to see me as abled. I want people to look at me and say, 'If she can do it, so can I.'

"I don't want any special attention. I just want people to see the same possibilities I do."

I'm such an advocate of life. After my accident, it came down to bitter or better, and I continuously work on choosing the latter. I don't ever want to be bitter again. I want to live open-minded, I want to ignore the limitations, I want to educate the masses. Sometimes we humans just need to know that somebody is rooting for us. I may not be playing on the field, but I'm not sitting on the bench, either. I am with the team on the sidelines cheering for everybody, my wheelchair shamelessly in tow.

"I think you're doing amazingly well," Kristen says. "I am so happy you keep choosing to never give up, Melissa. I'm so happy you still love me, and you still want to see me. I'm sorry I haven't been driving distance from you. You know how much I love you no matter what."

"Trust me, Kristen. It was extremely difficult the first couple of years. I know now to never put the blame on anybody else. I know we all had to pick up our own lives and move on. I only wish it hadn't taken me this long to get to a peaceful place. But day by day, I'm getting there. Thank you for sticking around. Thank you for never giving up on me, even when I gave up on myself. I can't tell you how thankful I am for the people who have not only stuck around but have also stepped in."

"Love never fails. Isn't that what you always say?" She smiles.

"Never forget it," I say. "Well . . . now that this amazing dinner has wrapped up, should we call Kaley? Do you want to go dancing? I'm not going to lie, Kristen: I am exhausted, but our visits are few and far between. I would love to pop it like it's hot with you guys tonight."

20
the hurt before
the healing

Music and dancing are very healing for me. I can't move much, but you'd better believe I'm going to move everything I have, which typically includes a lot of head and shoulders, and throwing in some bicep with my arms flying around. If that sounds like it would look funny, it probably does. But I love every minute of it! Sitting on a wheelchair, I see people's lower halves well before I see their faces. So if I'm going to be seeing people the rest of this life at butt-level, they might as well drop it low right next to me, yo.

So many people at the club come up to me and say they are so happy to see me out of the house. So many girls use my wheelchair as a prop in the middle of the dance floor. I crack up, and I go with it. I especially love it when guys come up and dance with me. That makes me feel like I fit in. I believe that dancing is not only a workout physically but also a salve emotionally. It breathes life into my soul. And believe it or not, my neck and shoulders are usually sore as heck the next day. I don't go out dancing too often, but when I do, I do.

I'm more free and open to whatever these days. I'm continuing to press on. It's a new day, and I am back here in the woods, reflecting on losses and gains.

Alicia, one of my aides, is sitting here with me. The sun is beaming off her curly black hair.

"Honestly, Melissa," she says, "I don't think I could ever be a quadriplegic. I like helping people too much. I can't imagine losing my ability to do that."

I chuckle and say, "Well, I haven't exactly stopped helping people. For me, it's just a little different. You know that. I think it's awesome that you enjoy helping people. I'm definitely grateful for your hands. For me, I do enjoy public speaking. I can't imagine not doing this right now with my life. I don't know where I'd be if this accident hadn't happened."

"Did you do a lot of bad things?" she asks.

"I mean, if I was out somewhere and there was alcohol available, it never scared me to drink it. I wasn't a bad person. I made the same decisions as the people I surrounded myself with."

She nods. "Peer pressure is real. I was always scared to make mistakes. It saved me from a lot of trouble, that's for sure. You and I are pretty different, but I think it's neat that God gave you another chance, and you recognized it."

"Yeah," I say with a smile. "I truly have gained so much more than I thought I had lost. My body is hurting, but my mind is working. I know for sure now that it's not about me—it's about helping everybody else."

"I feel the exact same way. How was last night with your friends?"

"Every time I'm with them, it feels as good as an oil change. I feel so 'normal' when I'm around people who see me as just that." I give Alicia a little smirk.

I'm feeling whole today. There are days, though, when it feels like something is missing. On those days, I sit back and think, Is there really something missing? Sure, I could name a thing or two, but when I shift my mindset, I realize how much is actually not missing. The body can be merely a physical distraction when our soul is suffering.

Alicia hasn't had it easy, either. I don't think anyone has. She lives with her husband but has no family locally. She moved away from everything she knew for love, and her time consists of working with me and being with her husband.

"I need more friends in my life," Alicia says. "We should go out again sometime. My birthday with you was a lot of fun." She giggles.

"I'm down. You just give me advance notice so I can figure out all the details, and we will make it happen."

One of the most important details I have to figure out is how to get places, since I can't drive anymore. Either I can schedule a public transportation ride twenty-four hours in advance, or a friend has to come and get me. So anything spontaneous doesn't really happen as often as my personality would like it to. On that note, though, life has definitely gotten easier. There's something about time and experience that can mold a grateful heart.

"What's on the agenda today?" Alicia asks, getting up from her camping chair.

"Well, I want to definitely do my workout, but afterward, I have a therapy appointment I'm looking forward to."

She giggles. "I have yet to meet a quadriplegic as active as you are. Sounds like a plan!"

"Oh, and could you please help me straighten my hair while I'm doing my electrical stimulation workout?"

"Of course," Alicia says. "Do you want me to grab anything else when I go inside?"

"Just my eyeliner, please. Thank you so much." I smile. I'm feeling energetic and ready for the day.

My hair has gotten so long over the years. I always had this dream of looking like a mermaid, with hair down to my hips. Mainly because I thought I could cruise around topless and no one would know, with all my hair in the way! That dream (not the topless one, but the long-hair one) has become a reality. I figure since a mermaid can't walk, either, might as well. So I have long blond hair that touches my thighs, and I love it. Cute hair and occasional eyeliner is all I want in this life!

Alicia is back and straightening my hair. She grabs a chunk and says, "I do have a question. Why don't you want a boyfriend?"

Oh, boy. This is the question everybody asks me. My friends think it's crazy that I haven't been in a serious relationship since my first breakup, which was roughly nine years ago.

There are so many things I could say, and there are many things on my heart, but I just say, "One breakup was enough."

I continue, "For years I would wake up and go through the day miserable and frustrated, constantly wondering when the pain was going to end. For the longest time, I had so much anger, and I'm still working on that."

Alicia slows down straightening my hair and looks at me curiously. "You know, honestly, Melissa, I wouldn't ever want to go through that kind of breakup, either. When my first boyfriend and I broke up, I never had to keep that reality next door to me. Not to mention my body has never stopped working, so I've never lost the freedom to physically move on. Have you healed from it?"

"Yes," I say. "What I didn't understand for years, but I do know now, is that my high school love and I were never going to work out, injury or no injury. We were never going to move in together, get engaged, much less get married. We were so young, just teenagers—we were adults legally but so far from mature. It was nothing short of bad timing. Wherever he ends up, I pray life treats him kindly."

My mind is racing. I normally try to avoid these memories, but now Alicia has me thinking. You can't go through touching a lover both physically and emotionally, and leave unchanged. It's just not possible. Humans crave each other. The satisfaction and affirmation that comes from somebody touching your heart in a way no one else ever has permanently changes you. And that's without an injury. When you're with the right person, you start to actually become the person you were meant to be.

It's amazing to me how crazy life is. Right after the crash, when I was struggling with my new paralysis, I didn't find the craziness so amazing, but now I find peace in it. It's like when you cross paths with someone who hurt you in the past, but your wound has healed, because you've become a better person. Or, on the flip side, maybe you meet someone whose touch leaves you breathless, and you know nothing could replace it. That's how crazy life is. And if that sounds intense, it is supposed to be. Love has this funny way of falling into place right before you think your life is about to fall apart. Because of that love, you entirely change how you interact with the world. Neither you nor anybody you know will ever be the same.

I tell Alicia, "I barely remember how a kiss feels. And that's okay, because in my heart I know God has somebody for me. Maybe we were never created exactly for one other person, but at the same time, what if we were? I don't know the answer to that. What I do know is everything we go through in life is an opportunity for us to grow. I have grown, and I have learned so much about finding the right person, and that's after only one breakup. I don't want to date multiple guys and get my heart repeatedly broken to understand the simple fact that waiting is worth it. I don't want to get intimate with multiple guys to feel needed. Sex was never made to be casual. Sex is a gift, and what a gift it is to give to somebody else, not *everybody else*, but somebody you don't ever want to let go of—in a much deeper way than ripping your clothes off will ever mean. The truth about love is that we all feel like if we give somebody everything, we will get everything we need back from them. It's scary to digest that that isn't exactly the truth. I want love so bad, and sometimes I think I will do anything for it."

Alicia looks thoughtful. "Well, Melissa, I think you need to start going out more and doing things to meet new guys. Your schedule is very busy. I know this from helping you. But I think between going to therapy appointments and speaking often, you're not getting out enough to meet new guys. I'm telling you, my husband is completely fine with me taking you out to do things off the clock, if you want to. Seriously, just let me know."

That makes my heart happy. I smile and say, "I want to find my guy. I want to make love last. I don't want to just give my body freely, hoping that the relationship ends up being more than how it started."

Alicia laughs. "Woah, tiger, slow down. I didn't say I'm trying to get you to lose everything you have been holding on to! All I'm saying is, let's go out; let's mingle with new guys. If there happens to be a guy you're interested in, then go from there. I think you're just playing it out too far in your head and freaking yourself out. I've seen guys check you out. Let's have fun with this."

"I promise, I'm not overthinking it," I say. "Well, I probably am! But I've seen how far it can go." I'm starting to get disheartened just talking about this. "I can't wait to feel wanted again. I can't wait until a guy looks me in the eye, wondering where I have been his whole life. The immense physical changes my body went through at eighteen left me extremely curious about how I could be a paralyzed girlfriend. Is it possible? I mean, is it? I got to know a few guys, along with all of their intentions, and I realized I couldn't force the answers to my questions. Back then, I woke up every morning and went to bed every night thinking about a romantic future. But I also knew that I didn't want to mess up anything else in my life to get it."

"Well . . ." Alicia looks as if she's wondering if it's even appropriate to say what's on her mind. "Are you still able to have a sexual relationship? I mean, does your body still work like that?"

I've been waiting for her to ask this. Because everybody does. I respond, "My body still works. I just don't have mental control of it. I can still have a full-term normal pregnancy, and I also get my menstrual cycle every month. Heck, you know, I'm on it right now! Some people think that just because I'm paralyzed, I don't want the same things a walking person does. That is a misconception. I still get the same feelings, the same urges, the same desires as any other female. The only difference is, I can't tell myself to physically stand up and act on it. My voice does work, though, and all I would have to do is tell somebody else how to handle my body. It really is that simple. And trust me, I have met numerous willing male counterparts."

Friends, family members, and so many caregivers are extremely curious and want to know "what it would be like."

And don't get me wrong, I can't wait to find out myself. I, too, am just as curious. Over time, though, I have developed mental strength and, I can tell you, I won't let my curiosity get the best of me. Just like anyone, I could easily act on it, finding out every answer to every question I have about my body.

It hasn't happened, though, because I haven't let it. I reassess my choice every day, and every day I choose not to act on it. It excites me to wait. It's thrilling to know that I'm saving this one body I have for only one more person. But at the end of the day, I am still human, and you'd better believe I can't wait for the day when AC/DC's "You Shook Me All Night Long" is more than just song lyrics in my life!

"Wow," Alicia says. "Honestly, people probably make assumptions because they just don't know. I can't wait to hear all about it, girl! I waited for my husband also. I honestly wouldn't have even given in to him if it hadn't felt so right. I know he's my soulmate. I also trust God, and I really respect my body. I think it's so awesome that you have waited this long."

I half smile and finish the conversation with, "I also think it's really cool you waited as long as you have. I hope you guys work out. It has been extremely hard for me to wait. I know my future husband will love to know that I don't need him but *want* him, more than anything. I can't imagine how amazing it would feel to hear from the man I love that he waited for me for as long as I've been waiting for him. So that motivates me to keep going, to keep waiting."

Alicia has finished straightening my hair, and even though we're done talking, my mind hasn't stopped running. Friends have bluntly told me that I won't find my husband unless I start dating. I do understand where they are coming from, but I'm not comfortable dating around, hoping to find him. I will eventually date somebody, but I just know in my heart I haven't come across the right somebody yet. I don't want to be the girl who has a boyfriend just so she doesn't feel lonely at night. I tried that before, and I don't want to try it again. I don't favor messing my life up any more than I was in favor of breaking my neck. I am on a journey of self-love. I'm craving to find out who Melissa really is—what she loves and what she can live without. I want to greet her with hope every morning.

I now know in order to truly live, you must give your life away. Believing doesn't make life perfect, it just makes it easier to handle. We weren't built to carry the weight that comes with shame, fear, anxiety, and guilt.

I'm surrendering. I'm no longer in the rut of depression I fell into after my mistake. I'm slowly reaching for a pure happiness, even in this paralyzed place.

I hear that they call that "grace."

21
lattes and love

So I propose a toast. Let's learn from people. It can never hurt to expand your mind. Everybody has something you can learn—the key is to never stop growing.

While I was living in the nursing home, a gentleman once told me that if you're the smartest person in the room, you're in the wrong room.

We have such a limited amount of time. I don't know about you, but I have no idea how much longer I get to be alive. You have to do what you love. If you're not doing it, or in some way pursuing it, the piercing ache won't go away until you speed up. We are supposed to be aching for more, because this life is only a taste. And what if this bittersweet taste is just a sample, just a mini-test to see what we can really handle? There's no grading scale, but WHAT IF not being able to control these weaknesses now ends up being something we miss out on later? My answer is, I don't know. The curious can only answer a question with a question. But still, what if . . .

So instead of blaming everything on the external, try to fight the internal, and realize we all have some learning to do. If it's not easy, you're on the right track.

I'm trying to dig deeper into the Bible and expand my understanding. In Genesis 32, Jacob goes through a physical change after wrestling with God. This is just one short biblical story that has grown on me. God had to leave Jacob with a physical reminder of a night that changed his life. I know now, I went through the same thing. I wrestled with God; my tears when I was in my coma told the story of me not wanting to come back to this life. I tried to dodge this bullet. Although quadriplegia is drastic, maybe I needed more than a hip out of socket to realize who I am in His name. I'm stubborn; sometimes I beg to differ that I know best. But what I'm learning more and more is that it's not about me, and it's not about getting a full physical healing. Just like God did with Jacob, He gave me a new name—Hope. And by golly, it is my job as His child to spread hope like wildfire.

I've spent countless hours at therapy appointments, and three to five hours at home doing my own therapy every day, but I haven't fully physically healed. Still,

I continue to work hard at it. Why? For one thing, I was never supposed to make the small yet significant recoveries I have. I've been admitted to the hospital only once in more than seven years. It's possible that I'm one of the few quadriplegics ever to have such a high level of injury and still be this physically healthy.

I don't boast. My heart is forever humbled. Because of the love I have received, I am extremely passionate about helping others with spinal-cord injuries. In fact, I recently have started up the Hope, Love, and Me Foundation.

The Hope, Love, and Me Foundation began from just that—hope and love. I started it with not just one but two goals. First, to increase my reach. The foundation helps me get to places as a motivational speaker that I would have been unable to get to without it. Places that need a little hope, places that need a sprinkle of motivation but are otherwise limited by budget constraints. Grace doesn't have a price, and with the aid of this foundation, I can now reach the unreachable.

Second, to encourage those in similar situations. This foundation helps me reach out to those who have also survived life-altering injuries. I help these people face the struggles and hardships of paralysis. It's hard to fight alone. I want to aid those who are injured—not only by showing them the road to mental recovery but also by showing them how to stabilize their physical health. Sometimes one just needs an advocate or a push in the right direction. I know I did. Humans have a right to fight for health, and sometimes we just need a little love to get through it. I want to help those struggling to pick up the pieces. I have a burning desire and vision to help millions, but I know I first must begin with just one.

Every morning when I wake up, I can't help but thank God for every bit of health and opportunity I have had. Between the fundraisers and the outpouring of love, my therapy has been continuous.

I'm headed to a therapy appointment now. I no longer feel dizzy or nauseated when I am upright out of my wheelchair. After the two to three hours at these appointments, I leave feeling rejuvenated. It would make sense if they made me feel tired, but it's actually the quite opposite. Getting out of my wheelchair makes me feel alive again. Weight-bearing with the use of therapeutic devices keeps not only my bones strong but also my mind. I feel like a new woman every time I wheel out of a therapy facility. Life just makes sense when I do things that make me feel good. I am absolutely committed. It doesn't matter how many hours I have to work on my injury; as long as God continues to give me chances, I will make use of them.

I used to rush through everything, anticipating the next climax. I didn't know it was already here, in every moment, even the ones that have the loudest silence. Hot lattes, pumpkin pies, and Jesus Christ are all what you make them. I'm choosing love, life, and light.

Speaking of lattes, there is this coffee shop two miles from my humble abode. I love everything about this place. The environment, people, and opportunities to mingle are just a few of the things that keep me coming back.

I'm not a caffeine addict yet (cue the BS alarm!). I guess I will admit it—maybe I am. Sometimes after a therapy appointment, I tell myself I deserve a treat. I'm convinced that often in life it's great to end working hard with a reward. But more often than not, I'm at the coffee shop first thing in the morning!

In fact, I'm coming through the front doors of this adorable place right now, and I'm headed straight to the order line. I have one thing on my mind, and that's a yummy twelve-ounce, single-shot latte. No flavor, and hold the sugar, please. I'm pulling up to the end of the line when, out of the corner of my eye, I see an old coworker from my grocery-store days. I haven't seen this guy in years. I'm an outgoing girl, but my injury has made me a little shy. Throughout the ten years of growing into the new me, I've been working really hard on pushing aside my fears of what people might think of the, well, wheelchair me.

It's easier when you can just walk around and blend in with the crowd of other walkers. I stand out, weird enough while sitting, even when I'm not wanting or trying to.

So I build up my courage, suck in a bunch of oxygen, and approach him.

"Oh, my gosh, Jason, how's it going? How have you been?" I say this like it's only been minutes since we last spoke. Really, we both know we don't know each other that well anymore. Work and mutual friends are what brought us together back in my two-working-legs days. We catch up with small talk, and it's not long before he introduces me to his friend, sitting directly across from him. I think I've seen this guy before.

"Melissa, this is my buddy Caleb," Jason says, beaming from ear to ear. Even when I worked with Jason, he was always smiling. I love it.

Caleb stands up to shake my hand, and his height has already got me all sorts of googly-eyed. I set my nonworking hand in his hand and tell him my name is Melissa. Come to find out, we go to the same church. Who knew? There's something cute about this guy. It's already my turn in line, so with a smile on my face, I tell them I'll see them around.

I'm starting to see the sexy in everybody, because there *is* a little bit of sexy in everybody. And although many cute guys work behind the counter here, my mind is still on the other tall something I just met and should've ordered! (Totally referring to Caleb, just in case you didn't pick up on that.) Wouldn't it be amazing if he decided to just come up to me before I left and say he wanted to get to know me? I wish guys were that comfortable with my disability.

I've had so many dreams of meeting a guy in a coffee shop and falling in love with him. There's something serene about a place that serves drinks that warm up not only your body but also your soul. I crave the kind of love that will blow my mind. God has my heart, and I'm trusting Him that at the right time, I will have my last first kiss. On that note, can somebody please give my guy a compass? He must be lost somewhere.

Broken bones heal, and so do broken hearts. I have worked hard to get to where I'm at mentally, and now I know that any life-changing event is just the beginning of a new adventure.

For some people, trusting God is easy. For others, it takes something big to force them to slow down, like me. And going through that can be the scariest thing.

I'm watching my milk get steamed, lost in thought, reminiscing about a rainy August night when my life changed. It was high school being over, it was a newly single relationship status, it was college starting in a week.

I had a plan; I thought I had it all figured out. But an unplanned night of drinking left me feeling emotionally drained, wanting to just get home and sleep in my own bed. Little did I know I was never going to actually make it there, and here I am.

It started with carelessly driving my Toyota Tundra, and now a wheelchair has replaced my body. But between all of the brokenness, I have a vision. I want to spread hope in such a way that one can't deny its existence. I want to fear only my next mistake, and find the will to not make it. I want love to take me deeper than my paralyzed body could ever wander.

As I'm wheeling out of the coffee shop, a couple opens the double doors for me. I look at them—I can tell they are so in love. My heart is beating out of my chest. The question is, where will this crazy life take me next?

I think I'm ready to let somebody sweep me off my feet—wait, I mean wheels.

where to get help

If you or someone you know has an acute or chronic spinal-cord injury, I recommend these facilities for inpatient/outpatient therapies:

The Shepherd Center
2020 Peachtree Road NW
Atlanta, Georgia 30309
Phone: 1.404.352.2020
www.shepherd.org

Kennedy Krieger Institute
The International Center for Spinal Cord Injuries
801 North Broadway
Baltimore, Maryland 21205
Phone: 443.923.9534
Toll Free: 888.923.9222

Fax: 443.923.9585
www.kennedykrieger.org

The Center of Recovery and Exercise
1191 Commerce Park Drive
Altamonte Springs, Florida 32714
Phone: 407.951.8936
Fax: 407.636.5235
www.coreflorida.com

If you or someone you know has an alcohol or narcotic addiction, there is help available. Check the websites for local chapters, or call the numbers below to get involved with Alcoholics or Narcotics Anonymous.

Alcoholics Anonymous World Services, Inc.
475 Riverside Drive at West 120th St. – 11th Floor
New York, NY 10115
Telephone: 1.212.870.3400
www.aa.org

Narcotics Anonymous World Services, Inc.
PO Box 9999
Van Nuys, California 91409
Telephone: 1.818.773.9999
Fax: 1.818.700.0700
www.na.org

If you or someone you know is depressed and wanting to take their own life, people care and are available. Visit the website below to chat with someone, or call the number for confidential support.

National Suicide Prevention Lifeline
Telephone: 1.800.273.8255
www.suicidepreventionlifeline.org

Crisis Text Line: Text HOME to 741741 for free, 24/7 crisis support in the U.S.
www.crisistextline.org

You have a story and a purpose. I believe in you.

acknowledgments

Where do I begin? Other than God being first and foremost, these are in no specific order. Well, except for the rents. To my mother that gave birth to me, and my stepfather that took us as a package deal . . . I will never be able to tell you enough how much I love you. Maybe one day I will have more than Social Security income to purchase you an island. Don't worry, mom; if that time comes, I will fill it with cheese and wine. To my brothers: thank you for being enough. I never dreamt of having a sister, because you guys made me feel so alive. Thank you for not disowning me, yet! To my biological father and every other family member near and far, I'm so grateful God gave me you. Have I told you the luck of me is Irish? To every friend, present, past, and future . . . you have contributed to who I am. At whatever stage of life you have known me or have come to know me, thank you for loving me. To every doctor, physical and occupational therapist, and any medical staff who have kept me physically going . . . Thank you! Because of your expertise and love for your fields, your girl is thriving. To every guy I had a crush on or even thought I had a chance with, thank you for keeping it sexy. To my future guy, get ready! I'm coming in hot. There truly is a little sexy in everybody. To every caregiver, oh, how I wish I could throw a big event and invite every single one of you. No matter how long you were a caregiver for me, I am grateful for your hands. A big thank-you to Stuart for believing in me, as well as helping me see this book through. If it wasn't for you, I wouldn't want to even know how this would have turned out. And lastly to this reader, you. I'm not sure why this life carries the amount of pain and beauty that it does. I'm not even sure of the mechanics or construction of how this life even happened. But I do know that is not for us to figure out. Get up, get going, and help people with every chance you get.

I can't wait to see where this life takes us.

~ Melissa Ann

about the author

Melissa Ann is Irish by blood, and paralyzed by grace. She aims to be an undercover agent one day, but figures the wheelchair stuck under her butt will blow her cover every time. So for now she is taking every opportunity to make a positive difference. By day she's a motivational speaker, and, by night, well, her parents are certain she's sneaking out of her bed. Melissa is partnered with the organization Mothers Against Drunk Driving, Hope Love and Me Foundation, and as many safety councils as she can muster. Her passion is lowering the amount of annual spinal-cord injuries that are caused by destructive choice making. She also gets out of bed on a daily basis to help people find hope in their own journey. She knows she can't save the world, but her goal is to help the people in it. Her assertive pup, TobyMac, will attack on demand if you try to get in the way of that. Now that, well, that's a service dog.

Godspeed.

www.HopeLoveAndMe.org
Instagram: @hopeloveandme